EX LIBRIS

VINTAGE **CLASSICS**

DYLAN THOMAS

Dylan Thomas was born in Swansea in 1914. He was the author of some of Britain's best-loved poems including 'Do not go gentle into that good night' and 'And death shall have no dominion', as well as the radio play *Under Milk Wood*. Although undistinguished at school Thomas began writing and publishing poetry as a teenager. After moving from Swansea to London in 1934 he published *18 Poems*, his first volume of verse. It was critically acclaimed and Thomas's reputation grew, both as a poet and as an exuberant personality. In 1937 he married Caitlin Macnamara and they moved to Laugharne, Wales, the town that would become the inspiration for the setting of *Under Milk Wood*. During the Second World War, Thomas was declared unfit for service and stayed in London, working as a scriptwriter and broadcaster for Strand Films and the BBC. He also continued to write collections of poetry and short stories as well as touring in the US. In October 1953 he returned for a fourth visit to America despite visibly poor health. He had spent much of that year revising *Under Milk Wood* but he died in New York before the BBC could record it. The first broadcast came two months later in January 1954 and starred Richard Burton. Dylan Thomas is buried in Laugharne.

DYLAN THOMAS

Under Milk Wood

A Play for Voices

WITH AN INTRODUCTION BY
Griff Rhys Jones

VINTAGE

1 3 5 7 9 10 8 6 4 2

Vintage Classics is part of the Penguin Random House group of companies
whose addresses can be found at global.penguinrandomhouse.com

Penguin
Random House
UK

Copyright © The Trustees for the Copyrights of Dylan Thomas 1954

Dylan Thomas has asserted his right to be identified as the author of this
Work in accordance with the Copyright, Designs and Patents Act 1988

First published in Great Britain by J. M. Dent & Sons Ltd in 1954
This paperback first published in Vintage Classics in 2024

Introduction copyright © Griff Rhys Jones 2024

penguin.co.uk/vintage-classics

A CIP catalogue record for this book is available from the British Library

ISBN 9781784878900

Typeset in 12/14.75 pt Bembo Book MT Pro by Jouve (UK), Milton Keynes
Printed and bound in Great Britain by Clays Ltd, Elcograf S.p.A.

The authorised representative in the EEA is Penguin Random House Ireland,
Morrison Chambers, 32 Nassau Street, Dublin D02 YH68

Penguin Random House is committed to a sustainable future for
our business, our readers and our planet. This book is made from
Forest Stewardship Council® certified paper.

MIX
Paper | Supporting
responsible forestry
FSC® C018179

Contents

Introduction

Despite its enticing opening, it is difficult to 'begin at the beginning' of *Under Milk Wood*. And possibly even more complicated to end at an ending.

Dylan Thomas had been commissioned to write his radio piece by the BBC in 1946. He eventually handed a late, deadline-serving version of it to his producer in November 1953. He wanted it straight back. He had scheduled a performance in New York. Dylan then left the invaluable, hand-scribbled pages in a pub. He was rushing across the Atlantic, in his usual scrambled way, just as he was rushing towards finishing his play. The producer, Douglas Cleverdon, thought it was 'very disordered', but managed to get a typescript to Thomas as he flew off.

Dylan then sat down and, under the strict supervision of his former army-captain New York mistress, banged out some final adjustments: key scenes and, indeed, an ending. They were handed to the American actors, as they stood waiting to go on stage for its 'premiere', ready to try out their Stateside Welsh accents. On the eve of a second full performance, with work possibly still in progress, there came the famous (and disputed) 'fourteen straight whiskies' calamity. Dylan Thomas fell ill and, without waking from a coma, died on 9 November 1953.

Now we might, as a result of this fitfulness and this tragedy, expect to find something inspired but unfinished, but *Under Milk Wood* is precise, and brilliantly crafted. This was not only the first, but, tragically, the last play that he ever wrote.

By 1953 Dylan Thomas was an international literary phenomenon. When *The Collected Poems* appeared, Philip Toynbee in *The Times* dubbed him 'the greatest living poet in the English language'. Nobody argued.

On the one hand, there is the dexterity of his poetry. Just as Matisse believed that colour represented raw emotion, so Dylan Thomas loved sonority. Someone once praised one of his poems. He asked them if they could identify the exact place that it was 'wrong'. He certainly could. He went to the two words that he felt had failed. To him, they were out of tune.

Now you may say this is no more than the work of any poet. But here, in the mix of spoken word, narration, parody and verse, this absolute precision, the pernickety intensity of choice, derived from his more 'serious' and allusive poetry, is applied to what is a largely prose piece of drama or even 'fun'.

Verse drama was briefly fashionable at the time, with T. S. Eliot's sombre plays and Christopher Fry's West End successes, like *The Lady's Not for Burning. Under Milk Wood* is barely acknowledged as belonging to that genre. Is this because it's funny? Is it because a lot of it appears to be in comic, conversational prose? It is hardly worth worrying about. On the one hand, it echoes Ben Jonson and his ornate, scatological London slang; on the other, it has the baroque verbal dexterity of P. G. Wodehouse (if not the silliness).

It is a poem. It is a play. It is an exploration of the power of language itself. Metaphors and similes, expressions, slang, vocal tics, rhymes and catchpenny phrases are plucked and put to work, to be read aloud and rolled around the tongue – sung out, recited, performed, relished.

Under Milk Wood had been bubbling away as an idea for a long time. Dylan Thomas was only seventeen when he first thought that idiosyncratic Welsh-village voices might make a play. Ten years later he told the author Richard Hughes that he had plans for a more fully formed work. He thought real villagers might even play themselves. He also told Hughes that he wanted to get some 'genuine madness' into it. He had an idea that the village could be 'certified mad' by the government. Later all outward references to the madness disappeared, though we might still detect the lunacy. It's the core of the characterisations of his villagers.

The final midwifery was protracted. Dylan Thomas returned from a fraught second tour of the States. He couldn't bring himself to settle to the introduction to his own collected poems. There were other promised pieces, too: such as a contract for a travel book about America, or the eagerly awaited first novel, which simply required an ending. He suffered a writer's block made of racing form, public bars and domestic chaos.

In 1949 he certainly started writing his final iteration in Laugharne (Welsh: Talacharn). On the radio, he described the Carmarthenshire seaside village as a place of '. . . feuds, scares, scandals, cherry-trees, mysteries, jackdaws in the chimneys, bats in the belfry, skeletons in the cupboards, pubs, mud, cockles, flatfish, curlews, rain, and human, often all too human, beings'.

This sounds like *Under Milk Wood* all right, but a semi-mythical 'heron-stalked, self-contained Welsh haven' had been part of Dylan's personal landscape for years. It's there in 'Poem in October', with its 'harbour and neighbour wood' and 'heron priested shore' and, critically, in the lines 'Myself to set foot that second in the still sleeping town'.

In *Quite Early One Morning*, a radio prose feature (written in 1945 in New Quay, or Cei Newydd in Welsh – another wood-shrouded, bay-enclosed village), he began with a town fast asleep (recognise it?) and then moved on to the voices of its separate residents, who included Mrs Ogmore-Pritchard. 'I woke up this morning' was as familiar a trope to Dylan Thomas as it was to Muddy Waters.

Under Milk Wood satisfied his earthbound inspiration – the same inspiration that he exercised writing and preparing scripts and radio presentations across the war years in London.

During this batch of unexpected, regular office work, Dylan Thomas wrote film scripts. He began to make use of his personal voice: his impersonations and parodies, the staples of his party-pieces and nightly saloon-bar, roaring-boy performances. Plans for feature films and whodunnits jostled with crazy murder mysteries, and even with one full script called *The Doctor and the Devils*. It was a dramatic education that must have influenced his accessible, tightly sprung first drama.

In 1948 he asked, 'Can we single out the amiably comic eccentricity of individual beings . . . when daily we are confronted, as social beings, by the dolt and the peeve and the minge and the bully, the maniac new atom? I prefer the attitude of Pepys: 12th Friday. Up, finding our beds good, but lousy; which made us merry.'

His 'Play for Voices' is a combination of the intensity of the poems and the roil of his comedy prose stories and, yes, jokes. 'It's organ organ all the time with him . . . up every night until midnight playing the organ,' says Mrs Organ Morgan and her neighbours.

Dylan liked to make pubs laugh. He punctured pomposity, sometimes to the point of embarrassment (once pretending to be a snarling dog in a lift and biting elderly posh people). He addressed po-faced students, 'I can't give a proper talk, but I might give an improper one.' When asked, at a stiffly formal party, what 'The Ballad of the Long-legged Bait' was really about, he replied loudly, 'a good fuck'. On his last trip to the US, the man who saw him off was not his publisher or his producer, but Harry Locke, a music-hall artist he admired for disrupting pubs with long, gibbering conversations in a pretend foreign language.

Dylan Thomas wrote his final revisions to *Under Milk Wood* with the sound of live laughter and applause in his ears. Doctor Theatre and the rewrite man played their part, but it's no afterthought that it was destined for the radio. He produced twenty-eight scripts for the wireless between 1943 and 1954. He called his play 'an entertainment out of the darkness'. He liked a listening audience – 'out there'. The piece exists in polyphonic limbo, with one voice blending into another.

As a result, of course, stage directors adore it. It is a blank page for any theatre. Seats, beds, cubbyholes, actors wandering all over the shop like a chorus – you name it. But if we go back to the original text, we find it using sound to reach across to us.

The blind central character, Captain Cat, takes over as narrator. He 'paints' with his poetic imagination. But in truth the whole play remains 'blind'. The voices continually invite us to see for ourselves:

Time passes. Listen. Time passes.
Come closer now.

Or 'Only you can hear.' Or 'Listen. It is night moving in the streets, the processional salt slow musical wind in Coronation Street and Cockle Row . . .'

As if we were under the bedclothes, inhabiting invisible blackness, Captain Cat's blindness creates sound for us: 'Waltzing up the street like a jelly, every time she shakes it's slap slap slap.' We can hear Mrs Dai Bread One coming, exactly as he does.

In truth, the village is full of noises. There are a few carefully chosen radio sound effects, marked as 'Noise of money-tills and chapel bells' for the love-struck shopkeepers Miss Price and Mr Edwards, but much of the jangle of the village is in the script itself. In just five lines we get 'the music of the spheres', a spring season that 'rustles', a glee-party that 'sings', dogs that 'bark', then there's 'a belch' and on we go.

The real sonority of *Under Milk Wood*, however, is in the speaking of it. If you happen to hear Dylan Thomas himself read, say, the famous poem 'And Death Shall Have No Dominion' (and it exists online), your expectations may be confused. It's a patrician tone. A full-blown, Forties, English-sounding 'radio' voice. It was said that he deliberately dropped an octave to perform.

Robert Hardy told Tom Hollander, who played Dylan in a film I produced, that as a very young actor he was introduced to the poet by Laurence Olivier. 'Hello, pleased to meet you,' said Thomas.

Hardy thought the pompous tone was Dylan joshing, so he answered with a silly voice himself. 'Pleased to meet you too-o-o.'

It was Dylan's 'normal' voice. And it is the voice he

employed when he read or presented on the BBC, not only reciting his own work, but also in renditions of Milton and Donne.

The singing of the words, the lilt, the tone were vital to him. He had no trace of a Welsh accent himself. Welsh people are often embarrassed by attempts to 'do' one. They can smell the fakery (as I have found to my cost, being brought up in Epping). The real Welsh accent varies widely from district to district, but the inherent musicality of intonation, the underlying rhythm that made my own English-toned father adopt a high pitched sing-song on the telephone, and which is always there in the 'posh' address adopted by Burton or Hopkins or Pryce, means that the sheer operatic clout of Anglo-Welsh lilt underlies the poetry in *Under Milk Wood*.

Dylan Thomas said in 1946, 'I've bored my wife to death for years by saying (among other things that have also bored her to death) that when you listen to poetry you should always be given an idea of the "shape" of the poem.' His great-uncle was a sermoniser, a preacher. The Welsh term 'hwyl', originally defined as a ship getting up speed under a full breeze, was translated into the emotional intensity of the pulpit and is the momentum of *Under Milk Wood*.

So, is Dylan Thomas too Welsh to be English, or too English to be properly Welsh? Most of Welsh Wales is bilingual. It does have a distinct 'English as she is spoken' voice. That is what we hear in *Under Milk Wood*. There is a Welsh English, and there is a south-west Wales English. These were his people speaking out as he, a non-Welsh speaker, experienced them.

It has been said (well, certainly by my own mother) that the Welsh are like the Italians. Is *Under Milk Wood* Fellini's *Roma*? We join an open, chatty forthright lot. They remind me of my own relatives, spread across the valleys of south Wales; would-be Ogmore-Pritchards and shopkeepers, farmers and ministers (not unlike Dylan's). He also had a list of Welsh references. They included 'hams on the hooks . . . cockles on the stalls, dressers, eisteddfodau, Welshcakes, slagheaps, funerals'. Amazing. They were my father's, too. Dylan had to look up the spelling of 'ach y fi'. As I would. It was a favourite expression of my grandfather's.

We feel his voice. We sense his hwyl. Lists have musicality. The names of cows ring like bells: 'Peg, Meg, Buttercup, Moll'.

Phrases are conversational surprises: 'the snip of a morning' or the sun 'cuffing the birds to sing'. The 'Voices', First and Second, the narrators, may be poetically elevated, as if on high, godlike, but once the daylight breaks in, the townspeople's talk is filled with an earthy, lilting articulacy:

> Oh there's a face!
> Where you get that hair from?
> Got it from an old tom cat.
> Give it back then, love.
> Oh there's a perm!
> Where you get that nose from, Lily?

Lily Smalls is gazing at herself in the mirror, prattling musically. The characters use songs, recitations and rhymes to express their fantasies and desires, but the detail of overheard, catchpenny gossip is continuous:

'. . . seen Polly Garter giving her belly an airing, there should be a law . . .'

The five hundred souls of Llareggub continually criticise and assess their fellow villagers. Even Captain Cat eavesdrops, and is funny with it:

'Mrs Floyd and Boyo, talking flatfish. What can you talk about flatfish?'

Across the Llareggub day, however, we are not just hearing these voices, but we are *overhearing* private dreams, secret conversations between couples, intimacies between mothers and sons, rituals shared between mistresses and servants. We are both omniscient and nosy, like Willy Nilly opening the post:

Mr Pugh . . . mixes especially for Mrs Pugh a venomous porridge unknown to toxicologists which will scald and viper through her until her ears fall off like figs, her toes grow big and black as balloons, and steam comes screaming out of her navel.'

The villagers have sophisticated, twentieth-century perversions, too, thank you. They enjoy their pettiness and relaxed bawdiness, their daring, their food and their sex. There is no solemn, Puritan working-class dignity in this community. It is a wholly tolerant 'madness'.

In a worksheet for the piece Dylan asked himself, 'what have I left out incest / greed / hate / envy?' The Fourth Woman says, 'There's a nasty lot live here when you come to think.' But we are not judgemental. We revel in vicissitudes and secret passions. Even ghosts, when we meet them, yearn for an unsophisticated joy:

> **SECOND DROWNED**
> Is there rum and laverbread?

> **THIRD DROWNED**
> Bosoms and robins?

> **FOURTH DROWNED**
> Concertinas?

> **FIFTH DROWNED**
> Ebenezer's bell?

> **FIRST DROWNED**
> Fighting and onions?

Drink, girls, food, songs and misbehaviour are what the drowned and the dead miss.

One character, Gossamer Beynon, teaches elocution – an echo of Dylan's own childhood. Childlike simplicity is one of the play's great strengths. Despite his own relish for sophisticated rhyme schemes, Polly Garter's lament or the Captain's song have a heartbreaking innocence reminiscent of Blake (a Dylan favourite). Interestingly, just before he wrote the final version, Dylan Thomas told Daniel Jones that *The Oxford Book of Nursery Rhymes* was close to hand.

Most of all *Under Milk Wood* is also a post-war celebration of life itself. Dylan had kept out of the war. He wanted to join the Peace Pledge Union to avoid conscription. (It told him that would have been more credible if he had joined before war was declared.) But he responded deeply to the bombing of Swansea and to the horrors of the atomic bomb and the deaths of children. Furthermore, the years immediately before *Under Milk Wood* had been full of personal loss. Thomas's father died from pneumonia just before Christmas 1952. In the first few months of 1953 his sister succumbed to liver cancer.

It is hardly surprising, then, that the drama seeks eternal verities. The day. The spring. Normality. Nature renewing itself. Drink is the daily escape. Life is settled, and is on an eternal self-contained round in Llareggub. It is of its time, but it's not going anywhere. In what was a hyperactive post-war world, it seems to know very little of, say, Aneurin Bevan, or the new Queen. Nobody is trying to escape to London and make their name.

Some have objected to this 'representation' of Wales. Is it fair? Is it just? Why should the Welsh be subject to such crude parody? But if Dylan Thomas had been more faithful to a balanced view of his fellow countrymen, with fewer comic exaggerations, I wonder if anyone would read this play now?

Thomas was sometimes down on his radio work for the BBC. In letters he called it 'blustering', 'hack-jobs', 'scriptlings' and 'radio-whinnie'. But he brought the same detailed attention to this, his final work, syllable by syllable, word by word, as he did to his poems.

This scrambled radio play has gone on living. A few years back, Peter Blake produced a fascinating illustrated edition. The Royal National Theatre went to a care home for a setting in 2022. Anthony Hopkins has directed it. Elton John and George Martin have composed music for it. Great actors have performed it – Michael Sheen, Siân Phillips, Peter O'Toole, Richard Burton, Elizabeth Taylor, Owen Teale, Rhys Ifans, Tom Hollander, Tom Jones, Alan Bennett and Charlotte Church. At the centenary I helped Jason Morell organise a well-attended Dylan festival with thirty-eight separate events across Fitzrovia. There will be more productions. *Under Milk Wood* has been nothing if not inspirational and yet remains entirely of itself: a first word, and, somehow, a last too.

Griff Rhys Jones, 2024

UNDER MILK WOOD

[*Silence*]

FIRST VOICE (*Very softly*)

To begin at the beginning:

It is spring, moonless night in the small town, starless and bible-black, the cobblestreets silent and the hunched, courters'-and-rabbits' wood limping invisible down to the sloeblack, slow, black, crowblack, fishingboat-bobbing sea. The houses are blind as moles (though moles see fine tonight in the snouting, velvet dingles) or blind as Captain Cat there in the muffled middle by the pump and the town clock, the shops in mourning, the Welfare Hall in widows' weeds. And all the people of the lulled and dumbfound town are sleeping now.

Hush, the babies are sleeping, the farmers, the fishers, the tradesmen and pensioners, cobbler, schoolteacher, postman and publican, the undertaker and the fancy woman, drunkard, dressmaker, preacher, policeman, the webfoot cocklewomen and the tidy wives. Young girls lie bedded soft or glide in their dreams, with rings and trousseaux, bridesmaided by glow-worms down the aisles of the organplaying wood. The boys are dreaming wicked or of the bucking ranches of the night and the jollyrodgered sea. And the anthracite statues of the horses sleep in the fields, and the cows in the byres, and the dogs in the wetnosed yards; and the cats nap in the slant corners or lope sly, streaking and needling, on the one cloud of the roofs.

You can hear the dew falling, and the hushed town breathing. Only *your* eyes are unclosed to see the black and folded town fast, and slow, asleep. And you alone can hear the invisible starfall, the darkest-before-dawn minutely dew-grazed stir of the black, dab-filled sea where the *Arethusa,* the *Curlew* and the *Skylark, Zanzibar, Rhiannon,* the *Rover,* the *Cormorant,* and the *Star of Wales* tilt and ride.

Listen. It is night moving in the streets, the processional salt slow musical wind in Coronation Street and Cockle Row, it is the grass growing on Llareggub Hill, dewfall, starfall, the sleep of birds in Milk Wood.

Listen. It is night in the chill, squat chapel, hymning in bonnet and brooch and bombazine black, butterfly choker and bootlace bow, coughing like nannygoats, sucking mint-oes, fortywinking hallelujah; night in the four-ale, quiet as a domino; in Ocky Milkman's lofts like a mouse with gloves; in Dai Bread's bakery flying like black flour. It is tonight in Donkey Street, trotting silent, with seaweed on its hooves, along the cockled cobbles, past curtained fernpot, text and trinket, harmonium, holy dresser, watercolours done by hand, china dog and rosy tin teacaddy. It is night neddying among the snuggeries of babies.

Look. It is night, dumbly, royally winding through the Coronation cherry trees; going through the graveyard of Bethesda with winds gloved and folded, and dew doffed; tumbling by the Sailors Arms.

Time passes. Listen. Time passes.

Come closer now.

Only you can hear the houses sleeping in the streets in the slow deep salt and silent black, bandaged night. Only you can see, in the blinded bedrooms, the combs and petticoats over the chairs, the jugs and basins, the glasses of teeth, Thou Shalt Not on the wall, and the yellowing dickybird-watching pictures of the dead. Only you can hear and see, behind the eyes of the sleepers, the movements and countries and mazes and colours and dismays and rainbows and tunes and wishes and flight and fall and despairs and big seas of their dreams.

From where you are, you can hear their dreams.

Captain Cat, the retired blind seacaptain, asleep in his bunk in the seashelled, ship-in-bottled, shipshape best cabin of Schooner House dreams of

SECOND VOICE
never such seas as any that swamped the decks of his S.S. *Kidwelly* bellying over the bedclothes and jellyfish-slippery

sucking him down salt deep into the Davy dark where the
fish come biting out and nibble him down to his wishbone,
and the long drowned nuzzle up to him.

FIRST DROWNED

Remember me, Captain?

CAPTAIN CAT

You're Dancing Williams!

FIRST DROWNED

I lost my step in Nantucket.

SECOND DROWNED

Do you see me, Captain? the white bone talking? I'm
Tom-Fred the donkeyman . . . we shared the same girl
once . . . her name was Mrs Probert . . .

WOMAN'S VOICE

Rosie Probert, thirty three Duck Lane. Come on up,
boys, I'm dead.

THIRD DROWNED

Hold me, Captain, I'm Jonah Jarvis, come to a bad end,
very enjoyable.

FOURTH DROWNED

Alfred Pomeroy Jones, sea-lawyer, born in Mumbles, sung like a linnet, crowned you with a flagon, tattooed with mermaids, thirst like a dredger, died of blisters.

FIRST DROWNED

This skull at your earhole is

FIFTH DROWNED

Curly Bevan. Tell my auntie it was me that pawned the ormolu clock.

CAPTAIN CAT

Aye, aye, Curly.

SECOND DROWNED

Tell my missus no I never

THIRD DROWNED

I never done what she said I never.

FOURTH DROWNED

Yes they did.

FIFTH DROWNED

And who brings coconuts and shawls and parrots to *my* Gwen now?

FIRST DROWNED

How's it above?

SECOND DROWNED

Is there rum and laverbread?

THIRD DROWNED

Bosoms and robins?

FOURTH DROWNED

Concertinas?

FIFTH DROWNED

Ebenezer's bell?

FIRST DROWNED

Fighting and onions?

SECOND DROWNED

And sparrows and daisies?

THIRD DROWNED

Tiddlers in a jamjar?

FOURTH DROWNED

Buttermilk and whippets?

FIFTH DROWNED

Rock-a-bye baby?

FIRST DROWNED

Washing on the line?

SECOND DROWNED

And old girls in the snug?

THIRD DROWNED

How's the tenors in Dowlais?

FOURTH DROWNED

Who milks the cows in Maesgwyn?

FIFTH DROWNED

When she smiles, is there dimples?

FIRST DROWNED

What's the smell of parsley?

CAPTAIN CAT

Oh, my dead dears!

From where you are you can hear in Cockle Row in the spring, moonless night, Miss Price, dressmaker and sweetshop-keeper, dream of

SECOND VOICE

her lover, tall as the town clock tower, Samson-syrup-gold-maned, whacking thighed and piping hot, thunderbolt-bass'd and barnacle-breasted, flailing up the cockles with his eyes like blowlamps and scooping low over her lonely loving hot-waterbottled body.

MR EDWARDS

Myfanwy Price!

MISS PRICE

Mr Mog Edwards!

MR EDWARDS

I am a draper mad with love. I love you more than all the flannelette and calico, candlewick, dimity, crash and merino, tussore, cretonne, crepon, muslin, poplin, ticking and twill in the whole Cloth Hall of the world. I have come to take you away to my Emporium on the hill, where the change hums on wires. Throw away your little bedsocks and your Welsh wool knitted jacket, I will warm the sheets like an electric toaster, I will lie by your side like the Sunday roast.

MISS PRICE

I will knit you a wallet of forget-me-not blue, for the money to be comfy. I will warm your heart by the fire so that you can slip it in under your vest when the shop is closed.

MR EDWARDS

Myfanwy, Myfanwy, before the mice gnaw at your bottom drawer will you say

MISS PRICE

Yes, Mog, yes, Mog, yes, yes, yes.

MR EDWARDS

And all the bells of the tills of the town shall ring for our wedding.

[*Noise of money-tills and chapel bells*]

FIRST VOICE

Come now, drift up the dark, come up the drifting sea-dark street now in the dark night seesawing like the sea, to the bible-black airless attic over Jack Black the cobbler's shop where alone and savagely Jack Black sleeps in a nightshirt tied to his ankles with elastic and dreams of

SECOND VOICE

chasing the naughty couples down the grassgreen gooseberried double bed of the wood, flogging the tosspots in the spit-and-sawdust, driving out the bare bold girls from the sixpenny hops of his nightmares.

JACK BLACK (*Loudly*)
Ach y fi!
Ach y fi!

FIRST VOICE
Evans the Death, the undertaker,

SECOND VOICE
laughs high and aloud in his sleep and curls up his toes as he sees, upon waking fifty years ago, snow lie deep on the goosefield behind the sleeping house; and he runs out into the field where his mother is making welsh-cakes in the snow, and steals a fistful of snowflakes and currants and climbs back to bed to eat them cold and sweet under the warm, white clothes while his mother dances in the snow kitchen crying out for her lost currants.

FIRST VOICE
And in the little pink-eyed cottage next to the undertaker's, lie, alone, the seventeen snoring gentle stone of Mister Waldo, rabbitcatcher, barber, herbalist, catdoctor, quack, his fat pink hands, palms up, over the edge of the patchwork quilt, his black boots neat and tidy in the

washing-basin, his bowler on a nail above the bed, a milk
stout and a slice of cold bread pudding under the pillow;
and, dripping in the dark, he dreams of

MOTHER

This little piggy went to market
This little piggy stayed at home
This little piggy had roast beef
This little piggy had none
And this little piggy went

LITTLE BOY

wee wee wee wee wee

MOTHER

all the way home to

WIFE (*Screaming*)

Waldo! Wal-do!

MR WALDO

Yes, Blodwen love?

WIFE

Oh, what'll the neighbours say, what'll the neighbours . . .

· 11 ·

FIRST NEIGHBOUR

Poor Mrs Waldo

SECOND NEIGHBOUR

What she puts up with

FIRST NEIGHBOUR

Never should of married

SECOND NEIGHBOUR

If she didn't had to

FIRST NEIGHBOUR

Same as her mother

SECOND NEIGHBOUR

There's a husband for you

FIRST NEIGHBOUR

Bad as his father

SECOND NEIGHBOUR

And you know where he ended

FIRST NEIGHBOUR

Up in the asylum

SECOND NEIGHBOUR

Crying for his ma

FIRST NEIGHBOUR

Every Saturday

SECOND NEIGHBOUR

He hasn't got a leg

FIRST NEIGHBOUR

And carrying on

SECOND NEIGHBOUR

With that Mrs Beattie Morris

FIRST NEIGHBOUR

Up in the quarry

SECOND NEIGHBOUR

And seen her baby

FIRST NEIGHBOUR

It's got his nose

SECOND NEIGHBOUR

Oh it makes my heart bleed

FIRST NEIGHBOUR
What he'll do for drink

SECOND NEIGHBOUR
He sold the pianola

FIRST NEIGHBOUR
And her sewing machine

SECOND NEIGHBOUR
Falling in the gutter

FIRST NEIGHBOUR
Talking to the lamp-post

SECOND NEIGHBOUR
Using language

FIRST NEIGHBOUR
Singing in the w

SECOND NEIGHBOUR
Poor Mrs Waldo

WIFE (*Tearfully*)
. . . Oh, Waldo, Waldo!

MR WALDO

Hush, love, hush. I'm *widower* Waldo now.

MOTHER (*Screaming*)

Waldo, Wal-do!

LITTLE BOY

Yes, our mum?

MOTHER

Oh, what'll the neighbours say, what'll the neighbours . . .

THIRD NEIGHBOUR

Black as a chimbley

FOURTH NEIGHBOUR

Ringing doorbells

THIRD NEIGHBOUR

Breaking windows

FOURTH NEIGHBOUR

Making mudpies

THIRD NEIGHBOUR

Stealing currants

FOURTH NEIGHBOUR

Chalking words

THIRD NEIGHBOUR

Saw him in the bushes

FOURTH NEIGHBOUR

Playing mwchins

THIRD NEIGHBOUR

Send him to bed without any supper

FOURTH NEIGHBOUR

Give him sennapods and lock him in the dark

THIRD NEIGHBOUR

Off to the reformatory

FOURTH NEIGHBOUR

Off to the reformatory

TOGETHER

Learn him with a slipper on his b.t.m.

ANOTHER MOTHER (*Screaming*)

Waldo, Wal-do! what you doing with our Matti?

LITTLE BOY

Give us a kiss, Matti Richards.

LITTLE GIRL

Give us a penny then.

MR WALDO

I only got a halfpenny.

FIRST WOMAN

Lips is a penny.

PREACHER

Will you take this woman Matti Richards

SECOND WOMAN

Dulcie Prothero

THIRD WOMAN

Effie Bevan

FOURTH WOMAN

Lil the Gluepot

FIFTH WOMAN

Mrs Flusher

WIFE
Blodwen Bowen

PREACHER
To be your awful wedded wife

LITTLE BOY (*Screaming*)
No, no, no!

FIRST VOICE
Now, in her iceberg-white, holily laundered crinoline nightgown, under virtuous polar sheets, in her spruced and scoured dust-defying bedroom in trig and trim Bay View, a house for paying guests, at the top of the town, Mrs Ogmore-Pritchard widow, twice, of Mr Ogmore, linoleum, retired, and Mr Pritchard, failed bookmaker, who maddened by besoming, swabbing and scrubbing, the voice of the vacuum-cleaner and the fume of polish, ironically swallowed disinfectant, fidgets in her rinsed sleep, wakes in a dream, and nudges in the ribs dead Mr Ogmore, dead Mr Pritchard, ghostly on either side.

MRS OGMORE–PRITCHARD
Mr Ogmore!
Mr Pritchard!
It is time to inhale your balsam.

MR OGMORE
Oh, Mrs Ogmore!

MR PRITCHARD
Oh, Mrs Pritchard!

MRS OGMORE-PRITCHARD
Soon it will be time to get up.
Tell me your tasks, in order.

MR OGMORE
I must put my pyjamas in the drawer marked pyjamas.

MR PRITCHARD
I must take my cold bath which is good for me.

MR OGMORE
I must wear my flannel band to ward off sciatica.

MR PRITCHARD
I must dress behind the curtain and put on my apron.

MR OGMORE
I must blow my nose.

MRS OGMORE-PRITCHARD
In the garden, if you please.

MR OGMORE

In a piece of tissue-paper which I afterwards burn.

MR PRITCHARD

I must take my salts which are nature's friend.

MR OGMORE

I must boil the drinking water because of germs.

MR PRITCHARD

I must make my herb tea which is free from tannin.

MR OGMORE

And have a charcoal biscuit which is good for me.

MR PRITCHARD

I may smoke one pipe of asthma mixture.

MRS OGMORE-PRITCHARD

In the woodshed, if you please.

MR PRITCHARD

And dust the parlour and spray the canary.

MR OGMORE

I must put on rubber gloves and search the peke for fleas.

MR PRITCHARD

I must dust the blinds and then I must raise them.

MRS OGMORE-PRITCHARD

And before you let the sun in, mind it wipes its shoes.

FIRST VOICE

In Butcher Beynon's, Gossamer Beynon, daughter, schoolteacher, dreaming deep, daintily ferrets under a fluttering hummock of chicken's feathers in a slaughterhouse that has chintz curtains and a three-pieced suite, and finds, with no surprise, a small rough ready man with a bushy tail winking in a paper carrier.

GOSSAMER BEYNON

At last, my love,

FIRST VOICE

sighs Gossamer Beynon. And the bushy tail wags rude and ginger.

ORGAN MORGAN

Help,

SECOND VOICE

cries Organ Morgan, the organist, in his dream,

ORGAN MORGAN

There is perturbation and music in Coronation Street! All the spouses are honking like geese and the babies singing opera. P.C. Attila Rees has got his truncheon out and is playing cadenzas by the pump, the cows from Sunday Meadow ring like reindeer, and on the roof of Handel Villa see the Women's Welfare hoofing, bloomered, in the moon.

FIRST VOICE

At the sea-end of town, Mr and Mrs Floyd, the cocklers, are sleeping as quiet as death, side by wrinkled side, toothless, salt and brown, like two old kippers in a box.

And high above, in Salt Lake Farm, Mr Utah Watkins counts, all night, the wife-faced sheep as they leap the fences on the hill, smiling and knitting and bleating just like Mrs Utah Watkins.

UTAH WATKINS (*Yawning*)

Thirty-four, thirty-five, thirty-six, forty-eight, eighty-nine . . .

MRS UTAH WATKINS (*Bleating*)

Knit one slip one
Knit two together
Pass the slipstitch over . . .

FIRST VOICE

Ocky Milkman, drowned asleep in Cockle Street, is emptying his churns into the Dewi River,

OCKY MILKMAN (*Whispering*)

regardless of expense,

FIRST VOICE

and weeping like a funeral.

SECOND VOICE

Cherry Owen, next door, lifts a tankard to his lips but nothing flows out of it. He shakes the tankard. It turns into a fish. He drinks the fish.

FIRST VOICE

P.C. Attila Rees lumps out of bed, dead to the dark and still foghorning, and drags out his helmet from under the bed; but deep in the backyard lock-up of his sleep a mean voice murmurs

A VOICE (*Murmuring*)

You'll be sorry for this in the morning,

FIRST VOICE

and he heave-ho's back to bed. His helmet swashes in the dark.

Willy Nilly, postman, asleep up street, walks fourteen miles to deliver the post as he does every day of the night, and rat-a-tats hard and sharp on Mrs Willy Nilly.

MRS WILLY NILLY

Don't spank me, please, teacher,

SECOND VOICE

whimpers his wife at his side, but every night of her married life she has been late for school.

FIRST VOICE

Sinbad Sailors, over the taproom of the Sailors Arms, hugs his damp pillow whose secret name is Gossamer Beynon. A mogul catches Lily Smalls in the wash-house.

LILY SMALLS

Ooh, you old mogul!

SECOND VOICE

Mrs Rose Cottage's eldest, Mae, peals off her pink-and-white skin in a furnace in a tower in a cave in a waterfall in a wood and waits there raw as an onion for Mister Right to leap up the burning tall hollow splashes of leaves like a brilliantined trout.

MAE ROSE COTTAGE
(*Very close and softly, drawing out the words*)
Call me Dolores
Like they do in the stories.

FIRST VOICE

Alone until she dies, Bessie Bighead, hired help, born in the workhouse, smelling of the cowshed, snores bass and gruff on a couch of straw in a loft in Salt Lake Farm and picks a posy of daisies in Sunday Meadow to put on the grave of Gomer Owen who kissed her once by the pig-sty when she wasn't looking and never kissed her again although she was looking all the time.

And the Inspectors of Cruelty fly down into Mrs Butcher Beynon's dream to persecute Mr Beynon for selling

BUTCHER BEYNON

owlmeat, dogs' eyes, manchop.

SECOND VOICE

Mr Beynon, in butcher's bloodied apron, spring-heels down Coronation Street, a finger, not his own, in his mouth. Straight-faced in his cunning sleep he pulls the legs of his dreams and

BUTCHER BEYNON

hunting on pigback shoots down the wild giblets.

ORGAN MORGAN (*High and softly*)
Help!

GOSSAMER BEYNON (*Softly*)
My foxy darling.

FIRST VOICE
Now behind the eyes and secrets of the dreamers in the streets rocked to sleep by the sea, see the

SECOND VOICE
titbits and topsyturvies, bobs and buttontops, bags and bones, ash and rind and dandruff and nailparings, saliva and snowflakes and moulted feathers of dreams, the wrecks and sprats and shells and fishbones, whalejuice and moonshine and small salt fry dished up by the hidden sea.

FIRST VOICE
The owls are hunting. Look, over Bethesda gravestones one hoots and swoops and catches a mouse by Hannah Rees, Beloved Wife. And in Coronation Street, which you alone can see it is so dark under the chapel in the skies, the Reverend Eli Jenkins, poet, preacher, turns in his deep towards-dawn sleep and dreams of

REV. ELI JENKINS
Eisteddfodau.

SECOND VOICE

He intricately rhymes, to the music of crwth and pib-gorn, all night long in his druid's seedy nightie in a beer-tent black with parchs.

FIRST VOICE

Mr Pugh, schoolmaster, fathoms asleep, pretends to be sleeping, spies foxy round the droop of his nightcap and pssst! whistles up

MR PUGH

Murder.

FIRST VOICE

Mrs Organ Morgan, groceress, coiled grey like a dor-mouse, her paws to her ears, conjures

MRS ORGAN MORGAN

Silence.

SECOND VOICE

She sleeps very dulcet in a cove of wool, and trumpet-ing Organ Morgan at her side snores no louder than a spider.

FIRST VOICE

Mary Ann Sailors dreams of

MARY ANN SAILORS

The Garden of Eden.

FIRST VOICE

She comes in her smock-frock and clogs

MARY ANN SAILORS

away from the cool scrubbed cobbled kitchen with the Sunday-school pictures on the whitewashed wall and the farmers' almanac hung above the settle and the sides of bacon on the ceiling hooks, and goes down the cockleshelled paths of that applepie kitchen garden, ducking under the gippo's clothespegs, catching her apron on the blackcurrant bushes, past beanrows and onion-bed and tomatoes ripening on the wall towards the old man playing the harmonium in the orchard, and sits down on the grass at his side and shells the green peas that grow up through the lap of her frock that brushes the dew.

FIRST VOICE

In Donkey Street, so furred with sleep, Dai Bread, Polly Garter, Nogood Boyo, and Lord Cut-Glass sigh before the dawn that is about to be and dream of

DAI BREAD

Harems.

POLLY GARTER

Babies.

NOGOOD BOYO

Nothing.

LORD CUT-GLASS

Tick tock tick tock tick tock tick tock.

FIRST VOICE

Time passes. Listen. Time passes. An owl flies home past Bethesda, to a chapel in an oak. And the dawn inches up.

[*One distant bell-note, faintly reverberating*]

FIRST VOICE

Stand on this hill. This is Llareggub Hill, old as the hills, high, cool, and green, and from this small circle of stones, made not by druids but by Mrs Beynon's Billy, you can see all the town below you sleeping in the first of the dawn.

You can hear the love-sick woodpigeons mooning in bed. A dog barks in his sleep, farmyards away. The town ripples like a lake in the waking haze.

VOICE OF A GUIDE-BOOK

Less than five hundred souls inhabit the three quaint streets and the few narrow by-lanes and scattered farmsteads that constitute this small, decaying watering-place which may, indeed, be called a 'backwater of life' without disrespect to its natives who possess, to this day, a salty individuality of their own. The main street, Coronation Street, consists, for the most part, of humble, two-storied houses many of which attempt to achieve some measure of gaiety by prinking themselves out in crude colours and by the liberal use of pinkwash, though there are remaining a few eighteenth-century houses of more pretension, if, on the whole, in a sad state of disrepair. Though there is little to attract the hill-climber, the healthseeker, the sportsman, or the weekending motorist, the contemplative may, if sufficiently attracted to spare it some leisurely hours, find, in its cobbled streets and its little fishing harbour, in its several curious customs, and in the conversation of its local 'characters', some of that picturesque sense of the past so frequently lacking in towns and villages which have kept more abreast of the times. The River Dewi is said to abound in trout, but is much poached. The one place of worship, with its neglected graveyard, is of no architectural interest.

[*A cock crows*]

FIRST VOICE
The principality of the sky lightens now, over our green hill, into spring morning larked and crowed and belling.

[*Slow bell notes*]

Who pulls the townhall bellrope but blind Captain Cat? One by one, the sleepers are rung out of sleep this one morning as every morning. And soon you shall see the chimneys' slow upflying snow as Captain Cat, in sailor's cap and sea-boots, announces today with his loud get-out-of-bed bell.

SECOND VOICE

The Reverend Eli Jenkins, in Bethesda House, gropes out of bed into his preacher's black, combs back his bard's white hair, forgets to wash, pads barefoot downstairs, opens the front door, stands in the doorway and, looking out at the day and up at the eternal hill, and hearing the sea break and the gab of birds, remembers his own verses and tells them softly to empty Coronation Street that is rising and raising its blinds.

REV. ELI JENKINS

Dear Gwalia! I know there are
Towns lovelier than ours,
And fairer hills and loftier far,
And groves more full of flowers,

And boskier woods more blithe with spring
And bright with birds' adorning,
And sweeter bards than I to sing
Their praise this beauteous morning.

By Cader Idris, tempest-torn,
Or Moel yr Wyddfa's glory,
Carnedd Llewelyn beauty born,
Plinlimmon old in story,

By mountains where King Arthur dreams,
By Penmaenmawr defiant,
Llareggub Hill a molehill seems,
A pygmy to a giant.

By Sawdde, Senny, Dovey, Dee,
Edw, Eden, Aled, all,
Taff and Towy broad and free,
Llyfnant with its waterfall,

Claerwen, Cleddau, Dulais, Daw,
Ely, Gwili, Ogwr, Nedd,
Small is our River Dewi, Lord,
A baby on a rushy bed.

By Carreg Cennen, King of time,
Our Heron Head is only
A bit of stone with seaweed spread
Where gulls come to be lonely.

A tiny dingle is Milk Wood
By Golden Grove 'neath Grongar,

But let me choose and oh! I should
Love all my life and longer

To stroll among our trees and stray
In Goosegog Lane, on Donkey Down,
And hear the Dewi sing all day,
And never, never leave the town.

SECOND VOICE

The Reverend Jenkins closes the front door. His morning service is over.

[*Slow bell notes*]

FIRST VOICE

Now, woken at last by the out-of-bed-sleepy-head-Polly-put-the-kettle-on townhall bell, Lily Smalls, Mrs Beynon's treasure, comes downstairs from a dream of royalty who all night long went larking with her full of sauce in the Milk Wood dark, and puts the kettle on the primus ring in Mrs Beynon's kitchen, and looks at herself in Mr Beynon's shaving-glass over the sink, and sees:

LILY SMALLS

Oh there's a face!
Where you get that hair from?
Got it from a old tom cat.
Give it back then, love.
Oh there's a perm!

Where you get that nose from, Lily?
Got it from my father, silly.
You've got it on upside down!
Oh there's a conk!

Look at your complexion!
Oh no, *you* look.
Needs a bit of make-up.
Needs a veil.
Oh there's glamour!

Where you get that smile, Lil?
Never you mind, girl.
Nobody loves you.
That's what *you* think.

Who is it loves you?
Shan't tell.
Come on, Lily.
Cross your heart then?
Cross my heart.

FIRST VOICE
And very softly, her lips almost touching her reflection,
she breathes the name and clouds the shaving-glass.

MRS BEYNON (*Loudly, from above*)

Lily!

LILY SMALLS (*Loudly*)

Yes, mum.

MRS BEYNON

Where's my tea, girl?

LILY SMALLS

(*Softly*) Where d'you think? In the cat-box?
(*Loudly*) Coming up, mum.

FIRST VOICE

Mr Pugh, in the School House opposite, takes up the morning tea to Mrs Pugh, and whispers on the stairs

MR PUGH

Here's your arsenic, dear.
And your weedkiller biscuit.
I've throttled your parakeet.
I've spat in the vases.
I've put cheese in the mouseholes.
Here's your . . .   [*Door creaks open*]
. . . nice tea, dear.

MRS PUGH

Too much sugar.

MR PUGH

You haven't tasted it yet, dear.

MRS PUGH

Too much milk, then. Has Mr Jenkins said his poetry?

MR PUGH

Yes, dear.

MRS PUGH

Then it's time to get up. Give me my glasses.
No, not my *reading* glasses, I want to look *out*. I want to see

SECOND VOICE

Lily Smalls the treasure down on her red knees washing the front step.

MRS PUGH

She's tucked her dress in her bloomers—oh, the baggage!

SECOND VOICE

P.C. Attila Rees, ox-broad, barge-booted, stamping out of Handcuff House in a heavy beef-red huff, black-browed under his damp helmet . . .

MRS PUGH

He's going to arrest Polly Garter, mark my words.

MR PUGH

What for, dear?

MRS PUGH

For having babies.

SECOND VOICE

. . . and lumbering down towards the strand to see that the sea is still there.

FIRST VOICE

Mary Ann Sailors, opening her bedroom window above the taproom and calling out to the heavens

MARY ANN SAILORS

I'm eighty-five years three months and a day!

MRS PUGH

I will say this for her, she never makes a mistake.

FIRST VOICE

Organ Morgan at his bedroom window playing chords on the sill to the morning fishwife gulls who, heckling over Donkey Street, observe

DAI BREAD

Me, Dai Bread, hurrying to the bakery, pushing in my shirt-tails, buttoning my waistcoat, ping goes a button, why can't they sew them, no time for breakfast, nothing for breakfast, there's wives for you.

MRS DAI BREAD ONE

Me, Mrs Dai Bread One, capped and shawled and no old corset, nice to be comfy, nice to be nice, clogging on the cobbles to stir up a neighbour. Oh, Mrs Sarah, can you spare a loaf, love? Dai Bread forgot the bread. There's a lovely morning! How's your boils this morning? Isn't that good news now, it's a change to sit down. Ta, Mrs Sarah.

MRS DAI BREAD TWO

Me, Mrs Dai Bread Two, gypsied to kill in a silky scarlet petticoat above my knees, dirty pretty knees, see my body through my petticoat brown as a berry, high-heel shoes with one heel missing, tortoiseshell comb in my bright black slinky hair, nothing else at all but a dab of scent, lolling gaudy at the doorway, tell your fortune in the tea-leaves, scowling at the sunshine, lighting up my pipe.

LORD CUT-GLASS

Me, Lord Cut-Glass, in an old frock-coat belonged to Eli Jenkins and a pair of postman's trousers from Bethesda

Jumble, running out of doors to empty slops—mind there, Rover!—and then running in again, tick tock.

Me, Nogood Boyo, up to no good in the wash-house.

Me, Miss Price, in my pretty print housecoat, deft at the clothesline, natty as a jenny-wren, then pit-pat back to my egg in its cosy, my crisp toast-fingers, my home-made plum and butterpat.

Me, Polly Garter, under the washing line, giving the breast in the garden to my bonny new baby. Nothing grows in our garden, only washing. And babies. And where's their fathers live, my love? Over the hills and far away. You're looking up at me now. I know what you're thinking, you poor little milky creature. You're thinking, you're no better than you should be, Polly, and that's good enough for me. Oh, isn't life a terrible thing, thank God?

[*Single long high chord on strings*]

Now frying-pans spit, kettles and cats purr in the kitchen. The town smells of seaweed and breakfast all the way down from Bay View, where Mrs Ogmore-Pritchard, in smock and turban, big-besomed to engage the dust, picks at her starch-less bread and sips lemon-rind tea, to Bottom Cottage, where Mr Waldo, in bowler and bib, gobbles his bubble-and-squeak and kippers and swigs from the saucebottle. Mary Ann Sailors

MARY ANN SAILORS

praises the Lord who made porridge.

FIRST VOICE

Mr Pugh

MR PUGH

remembers ground glass as he juggles his omelet.

FIRST VOICE

Mrs Pugh

MRS PUGH

nags the salt-cellar.

FIRST VOICE

Willy Nilly postman

WILLY NILLY

downs his last bucket of black brackish tea and rumbles out bandy to the clucking back where the hens twitch and grieve for their tea-soaked sops.

FIRST VOICE

Mrs Willy Nilly

MRS WILLY NILLY

full of tea to her double-chinned brim broods and bub-
bles over her coven of kettles on the hissing hot range always
ready to steam open the mail.

FIRST VOICE

The Reverend Eli Jenkins

REV. ELI JENKINS

finds a rhyme and dips his pen in his cocoa.

FIRST VOICE

Lord Cut-Glass in his ticking kitchen

LORD CUT-GLASS

scampers from clock to clock, a bunch of clock-keys in
one hand, a fish-head in the other.

FIRST VOICE

Captain Cat in his galley

CAPTAIN CAT

blind and fine-fingered savours his sea-fry.

Mr and Mrs Cherry Owen, in their Donkey Street room that is bedroom, parlour, kitchen, and scullery, sit down to last night's supper of onions boiled in their overcoats and broth of spuds and baconrind and leeks and bones.

MRS CHERRY OWEN

See that smudge on the wall by the picture of Auntie Blossom? That's where you threw the sago.

[*Cherry Owen laughs with delight*]

MRS CHERRY OWEN

You only missed me by a inch.

CHERRY OWEN

I always miss Auntie Blossom too.

MRS CHERRY OWEN

Remember last night? In you reeled, my boy, as drunk as a deacon with a big wet bucket and a fish-frail full of stout and you looked at me and you said, 'God has come home!' you said, and then over the bucket you went, sprawling and bawling, and the floor was all flagons and eels.

CHERRY OWEN

Was I wounded?

MRS CHERRY OWEN

And then you took off your trousers and you said, 'Does anybody want a fight!' Oh, you old baboon.

CHERRY OWEN

Give me a kiss.

MRS CHERRY OWEN

And then you sang 'Bread of Heaven,' tenor and bass.

CHERRY OWEN

I *always* sing 'Bread of Heaven.'

MRS CHERRY OWEN

And then you did a little dance on the table.

CHERRY OWEN

I did?

MRS CHERRY OWEN

Drop dead!

CHERRY OWEN

And then what did I do?

MRS CHERRY OWEN

Then you cried like a baby and said you were a poor
drunk orphan with nowhere to go but the grave.

CHERRY OWEN

And what did I do next, my dear?

MRS CHERRY OWEN

Then you danced on the table all over again and said you
were King Solomon Owen and I was your Mrs Sheba.

CHERRY OWEN (*Softly*)

And then?

MRS CHERRY OWEN

And then I got you into bed and you snored all night like
a brewery.

[*Mr and Mrs Cherry Owen laugh delightedly together*]

FIRST VOICE

From Beynon Butchers in Coronation Street, the smell
of fried liver sidles out with onions on its breath. And listen!
In the dark breakfast-room behind the shop, Mr and Mrs
Beynon, waited upon by their treasure, enjoy, between bites,
their everymorning hullabaloo, and Mrs Beynon slips the
gristly bits under the tasselled tablecloth to her fat cat.

[*Cat purrs*]

MRS BEYNON

She likes the liver, Ben.

MR BEYNON

She ought to do, Bess. It's her brother's.

MRS BEYNON (*Screaming*)

Oh, d'you hear that, Lily?

LILY SMALLS

Yes, mum.

MRS BEYNON

We're eating pusscat.

LILY SMALLS

Yes, mum.

MRS BEYNON

Oh, you cat-butcher!

MR BEYNON

It was doctored, mind.

MRS BEYNON (*Hysterical*)

What's that got to do with it?

MR BEYNON

Yesterday we had mole.

MRS BEYNON

Oh, Lily, Lily!

MR BEYNON

Monday, otter. Tuesday, shrews.

[*Mrs Beynon screams*]

LILY SMALLS

Go on, Mrs Beynon. He's the biggest liar in town.

MRS BEYNON

Don't you dare say that about Mr Beynon.

LILY SMALLS

Everybody knows it, mum.

MRS BEYNON

Mr Beynon never tells a lie. Do you, Ben?

MR BEYNON

No, Bess. And now I am going out after the corgies, with my little cleaver.

MRS BEYNON

Oh, Lily, Lily!

Up the street, in the Sailors Arms, Sinbad Sailors, grandson of Mary Ann Sailors, draws a pint in the sunlit bar. The ship's clock in the bar says half past eleven. Half past eleven is opening time. The hands of the clock have stayed still at half past eleven for fifty years. It is always opening time in the Sailors Arms.

SINBAD

Here's to me, Sinbad.

FIRST VOICE

All over the town, babies and old men are cleaned and put into their broken prams and wheeled on to the sunlit cockled cobbles or out into the backyards under the dancing underclothes, and left. A baby cries.

OLD MAN

I want my pipe and he wants his bottle.

[*School bell rings*]

FIRST VOICE

Noses are wiped, heads picked, hair combed, paws scrubbed, ears boxed, and the children shrilled off to school.

SECOND VOICE

Fishermen grumble to their nets. Nogood Boyo goes out in the dinghy *Zanzibar,* ships the oars, drifts slowly in the dab-filled bay, and, lying on his back in the unbaled water, among crabs' legs and tangled lines, looks up at the spring sky.

NOGOOD BOYO (*Softly, lazily*)
I don't know who's up there and I don't care.

FIRST VOICE
He turns his head and looks up at Llareggub Hill, and sees, among green lathered trees, the white houses of the strewn away farms, where farmboys whistle, dogs shout, cows low, but all too far away for him, or you, to hear. And in the town, the shops squeak open. Mr Edwards, in butterfly-collar and straw-hat at the doorway of Manchester House, measures with his eye the dawdlers-by for striped flannel shirts and shrouds and flowery blouses, and bellows to himself in the darkness behind his eye

MR EDWARDS (*Whispers*)
I love Miss Price.

FIRST VOICE
Syrup is sold in the post-office. A car drives to market, full of fowls and a farmer. Milk-churns stand at Coronation Corner like short silver policemen. And, sitting at the open window of Schooner House, blind Captain Cat hears all the morning of the town.

[*School bell in background. Children's voices.
The noise of children's feet on the cobbles*]

CAPTAIN CAT (*Softly, to himself*)

Maggie Richards, Ricky Rhys, Tommy Powell, our Sal, little Gerwain, Billy Swansea with the dog's voice, one of Mr Waldo's, nasty Humphrey, Jackie with the sniff ... Where's Dicky's Albie? and the boys from Ty-pant? Perhaps they got the rash again.

[*A sudden cry among the children's voices*]

CAPTAIN CAT

Somebody's hit Maggie Richards. Two to one it's Billy Swansea. Never trust a boy who barks.

[*A burst of yelping crying*]

Right again! It's Billy.

FIRST VOICE

And the children's voices cry away.

[*Postman's rat-a-tat on door, distant*]

CAPTAIN CAT (*Softly, to himself*)

That's Willy Nilly knocking at Bay View. Rat-a-tat, very soft. The knocker's got a kid glove on. Who's sent a letter to Mrs Ogmore-Pritchard?

[*Rat-a-tat, distant again*]

CAPTAIN CAT

Careful now, she swabs the front glassy. Every step's like a bar of soap. Mind your size twelveses. That old Bessie would beeswax the lawn to make the birds slip.

WILLY NILLY

Morning, Mrs Ogmore-Pritchard.

MRS OGMORE-PRITCHARD

Good morning, postman.

WILLY NILLY

Here's a letter for you with stamped and addressed envelope enclosed, all the way from Builth Wells. A gentleman wants to study birds and can he have accommodation for two weeks and a bath vegetarian.

MRS OGMORE-PRITCHARD

No.

WILLY NILLY (*Persuasively*)

You wouldn't know he was in the house, Mrs Ogmore-Pritchard. He'd be out in the mornings at the bang of dawn with his bag of breadcrumbs and his little telescope . . .

MRS OGMORE-PRITCHARD

And come home at all hours covered with feathers. I don't want persons in my nice clean rooms breathing all over the chairs . . .

WILLY NILLY

Cross my heart, he won't breathe.

MRS OGMORE-PRITCHARD

. . . and putting their feet on my carpets and sneezing on my china and sleeping in my sheets . . .

WILLY NILLY

He only wants a *single* bed, Mrs Ogmore-Pritchard.

[*Door slams*]

CAPTAIN CAT (*Softly*)

And back she goes to the kitchen to polish the potatoes.

FIRST VOICE

Captain Cat hears Willy Nilly's feet heavy on the distant cobbles.

CAPTAIN CAT

One, two, three, four, five . . . That's Mrs Rose Cottage. What's today? Today she gets the letter from her sister in Gorslas. How's the twins' teeth?

He's stopping at School House.

WILLY NILLY

Morning, Mrs Pugh. Mrs Ogmore-Pritchard won't have a gentleman in from Builth Wells because he'll sleep in her sheets, Mrs Rose Cottage's sister in Gorslas's twins have got to have them out . . .

MRS PUGH

Give me the parcel.

WILLY NILLY

It's for *Mr* Pugh, Mrs Pugh.

MRS PUGH

Never you mind. What's inside it?

WILLY NILLY

A book called *Lives of the Great Poisoners*.

CAPTAIN CAT

That's Manchester House.

WILLY NILLY

Morning, Mr Edwards. Very small news. Mrs Ogmore-Pritchard won't have birds in the house, and Mr Pugh's bought a book now on how to do in Mrs Pugh.

MR EDWARDS

Have you got a letter from *her*?

WILLY NILLY

Miss Price loves you with all her heart. Smelling of lavender today. She's down to the last of the elderflower wine but the quince jam's bearing up and she's knitting roses on the doilies. Last week she sold three jars of boiled sweets, pound of humbugs, half a box of jellybabies and six coloured photos of Llareggub. Yours for ever. Then twenty-one X's.

MR EDWARDS

Oh, Willy Nilly, she's a ruby! Here's my letter. Put it into her hands now.

[*Slow feet on cobbles, quicker feet approaching*]

CAPTAIN CAT

Mr Waldo hurrying to the Sailors Arms. Pint of stout with a egg in it.   [*Footsteps stop*]

(*Softly*) There's a letter for him.

WILLY NILLY

It's another paternity summons, Mr Waldo.

FIRST VOICE

The quick footsteps hurry on along the cobbles and up three steps to the Sailors Arms.

MR WALDO (*Calling out*)

Quick, Sinbad. Pint of stout. And no egg in.

FIRST VOICE

People are moving now up and down the cobbled street.

CAPTAIN CAT

All the women are out this morning, in the sun. You can tell it's Spring. There goes Mrs Cherry, you can tell her by her trotters, off she trots new as a daisy. Who's that talking by the pump? Mrs Floyd and Boyo, talking flatfish. What can you talk about flatfish? That's Mrs Dai Bread One, waltzing up the street like a jelly, every time she shakes it's slap slap slap. Who's that? Mrs Butcher Beynon with her pet black cat, it follows her everywhere, miaow and all. There goes Mrs Twenty-Three, important, the sun gets up and goes down in her dewlap, when she shuts her eyes, it's night. High heels now, in the morning too, Mrs Rose Cottage's eldest Mae, seventeen and never been kissed ho ho, going young and milking under my window to the field with the nanny-goats, she reminds me all the way. Can't hear what the women are gabbing round the pump. Same as ever. Who's having a baby, who blacked whose eye, seen Polly Garter giving her belly an airing, there should be a law, seen Mrs Beynon's new mauve jumper, it's her old grey jumper dyed, who's dead, who's dying, there's a lovely day, oh the cost of soapflakes!

[*Organ music, distant*]

CAPTAIN CAT

Organ Morgan's at it early. You can tell it's Spring.

FIRST VOICE

And he hears the noise of milk-cans.

CAPTAIN CAT

Ocky Milkman on his round. I will say this, his milk's as fresh as the dew. Half dew it is. Snuffle on, Ocky, watering the town . . . Somebody's coming. Now the voices round the pump can see somebody coming. Hush, there's a hush! You can tell by the noise of the hush, it's Polly Garter. (*Louder*) Hullo, Polly, who's there?

POLLY GARTER (*Off*)

Me, love.

CAPTAIN CAT

That's Polly Garter. (*Softly*) Hullo, Polly my love, can you hear the dumb goose-hiss of the wives as they huddle and peck or flounce at a waddle away? Who cuddled you when? Which of their gandering hubbies moaned in Milk Wood for your naughty mothering arms and body like a wardrobe, love? Scrub the floors of the Welfare Hall for the Mothers' Union Social Dance, you're one mother won't wriggle her roly poly bum or pat her fat little buttery feet in that wedding-ringed holy tonight though the waltzing breadwinners snatched from the cosy smoke of the Sailors Arms will grizzle and mope.

[*A cock crows*]

CAPTAIN CAT

Too late, cock, too late

SECOND VOICE

for the town's half over with its morning. The morning's busy as bees.

[*Organ music fades into silence*]

FIRST VOICE

There's the clip clop of horses on the sunhoneyed cobbles of the humming streets, hammering of horseshoes, gobble quack and cackle, tomtit twitter from the bird-ounced boughs, braying on Donkey Down. Bread is baking, pigs are grunting, chop goes the butcher, milk-churns bell, tills ring, sheep cough, dogs shout, saws sing. Oh, the Spring whinny and morning moo from the clog dancing farms, the gulls' gab and rabble on the boat-bobbing river and sea and the cockles bubbling in the sand, scamper of sanderlings, curlew cry, crow caw, pigeon coo, clock strike, bull bellow, and the ragged gabble of the beargarden school as the women scratch and babble in Mrs Organ Morgan's general shop where everything is sold: custard, buckets, henna, rat-traps, shrimp-nets, sugar, stamps, confetti, paraffin, hatchets, whistles.

FIRST WOMAN

Mrs Ogmore-Pritchard

SECOND WOMAN

la di da

FIRST WOMAN

got a man in Builth Wells

THIRD WOMAN

and he got a little telescope to look at birds

SECOND WOMAN

Willy Nilly said

THIRD WOMAN

Remember her first husband? He didn't need a telescope

FIRST WOMAN

he looked at them undressing through the keyhole

THIRD WOMAN

and he used to shout Tallyho

SECOND WOMAN

but Mr Ogmore was a proper gentleman

FIRST WOMAN

even though he hanged his collie.

THIRD WOMAN

Seen Mrs Butcher Beynon?

SECOND WOMAN

she said Butcher Beynon put dogs in the mincer

FIRST WOMAN

go on, he's pulling her leg

THIRD WOMAN

now don't you dare tell her that, there's a dear

SECOND WOMAN

or she'll think he's trying to pull it off and eat it.

FOURTH WOMAN

There's a nasty lot live here when you come to think.

FIRST WOMAN

Look at that Nogood Boyo now

SECOND WOMAN

too lazy to wipe his snout

THIRD WOMAN

and going out fishing every day and all he ever brought back was a Mrs Samuels

FIRST WOMAN

been in the water a week.

SECOND WOMAN

And look at Ocky Milkman's wife that nobody's ever seen

FIRST WOMAN

he keeps her in the cupboard with the empties

THIRD WOMAN

and think of Dai Bread with two wives

SECOND WOMAN

one for the daytime one for the night.

FOURTH WOMAN

Men are brutes on the quiet.

THIRD WOMAN

And how's Organ Morgan, Mrs Morgan?

FIRST WOMAN

you look dead beat

SECOND WOMAN

it's organ organ all the time with him

THIRD WOMAN

up every night until midnight playing the organ.

MRS ORGAN MORGAN

Oh, I'm a martyr to music.

FIRST VOICE

Outside, the sun springs down on the rough and tumbling town. It runs through the hedges of Goosegog Lane, cuffing the birds to sing. Spring whips green down Cockle Row, and the shells ring out. Llareggub this snip of a morning is wildfruit and warm, the streets, fields, sands and waters springing in the young sun.

SECOND VOICE

Evans the Death presses hard with black gloves on the coffin of his breast in case his heart jumps out.

EVANS THE DEATH (*Harshly*)

Where's your dignity. Lie down.

SECOND VOICE

Spring stirs Gossamer Beynon schoolmistress like a spoon.

GOSSAMER BEYNON (*Tearfully*)

Oh, what can I do? I'll *never* be refined if I twitch.

SECOND VOICE

Spring this strong morning foams in a flame in Jack Black as he cobbles a high-heeled shoe for Mrs Dai Bread Two the gypsy, but he hammers it sternly out.

JACK BLACK (*To a hammer rhythm*)

There is *no leg* belonging to the foot that belongs to this shoe.

SECOND VOICE

The sun and the green breeze ship Captain Cat sea-memory again.

CAPTAIN CAT

No, *I'll* take the mulatto, by God, who's captain here? Parlez-vous jig jig, Madam?

SECOND VOICE

Mary Ann Sailors says very softly to herself as she looks out at Llareggub Hill from the bedroom where she was born

MARY ANN SAILORS (*Loudly*)

It is Spring in Llareggub in the sun in my old age, and this is the Chosen Land.

[*A choir of children's voices suddenly cries out on one, high, glad, long, sighing note*]

FIRST VOICE

And in Willy Nilly the Postman's dark and sizzling damp tea-coated misty pygmy kitchen where the spittingcat kettles throb and hop on the range, Mrs Willy Nilly steams open Mr Mog Edwards' letter to Miss Myfanwy Price and reads it aloud to Willy Nilly by the squint of the Spring sun through the one sealed window running with tears, while the drugged, bedraggled hens at the back door whimper and snivel for the lickerish bog-black tea.

MRS WILLY NILLY

From Manchester House, Llareggub. Sole Prop: Mr Mog Edwards (late of Twll), Linendraper, Haberdasher, Master Tailor, Costumier. For West End Negligee, Lingerie, Teagowns, Evening Dress, Trousseaux, Layettes. Also Ready to Wear for All Occasions. Economical Outfitting for Agricultural Employment Our Speciality, Wardrobes Bought. Among Our Satisfied Customers Ministers of Religion and J.P's. Fittings by Appointment. Advertising Weekly in the *Twll Bugle*. Beloved Myfanwy Price my Bride in Heaven,

MOG EDWARDS

I love you until Death do us part and then we shall be together for ever and ever. A new parcel of ribbons has come from Carmarthen today, all the colours in the rainbow. I wish I could tie a ribbon in your hair a white one but it cannot be. I dreamed last night you were all dripping wet and you sat on my lap as the Reverend Jenkins went down the street. I see you got a mermaid in your lap he said and he lifted his hat. He is a proper Christian. Not like Cherry Owen who said you should have thrown her back he said. Business is very poorly. Polly Garter bought two garters with roses but she never got stockings so what is the use I say. Mr Waldo tried to sell me a woman's nightie outsize he said he found it and we know where. I sold a packet of pins to Tom the Sailors to pick his teeth. If this goes on I shall be in the workhouse. My heart is in your bosom and yours is in mine. God be with you always Myfanwy Price and keep you lovely for me in His Heavenly Mansion. I must stop now and remain, Your Eternal, Mog Edwards.

MRS WILLY NILLY

And then a little message with a rubber stamp. Shop at Mog's!!!

FIRST VOICE

And Willy Nilly, rumbling, jockeys out again to the three-seated shack called the House of Commons in the back where the hens weep, and sees, in sudden Springshine,

SECOND VOICE

herring gulls heckling down to the harbour where the fishermen spit and prop the morning up and eye the fishy sea smooth to the sea's end as it lulls in blue. Green and gold money, tobacco, tinned salmon, hats with feathers, pots of fish-paste, warmth for the winter-to-be, weave and leap in it rich and slippery in the flash and shapes of fishes through the cold sea-streets. But with blue lazy eyes the fishermen gaze at that milkmaid whispering water with no ruck or ripple as though it blew great guns and serpents and typhooned the town.

FISHERMAN

Too rough for fishing today.

SECOND VOICE

And they thank God, and gob at a gull for luck, and moss-slow and silent make their way uphill, from the still still sea, towards the Sailors Arms as the children

[*School bell*]

FIRST VOICE

spank and scamper rough and singing out of school into the draggletail yard. And Captain Cat at his window says soft to himself the words of their song.

CAPTAIN CAT (*To the beat of the singing*)

Johnnie Crack and Flossie Snail
Kept their baby in a milking pail
Flossie Snail and Johnnie Crack
One would pull it out and one would put it back

O it's my turn now said Flossie Snail
To take the baby from the milking pail
And it's my turn now said Johnnie Crack
To smack it on the head and put it back

Johnnie Crack and Flossie Snail
Kept their baby in a milking pail
One would put it back and one would pull it out

And all it had to drink was ale and stout
For Johnnie Crack and Flossie Snail
Always used to say that stout and ale
Was *good* for a baby in a milking pail.

[*Long pause*]

FIRST VOICE

The music of the spheres is heard distinctly over Milk Wood. It is 'The Rustle of Spring'.

SECOND VOICE

A glee-party sings in Bethesda Graveyard, gay but muffled.

FIRST VOICE

Vegetables make love above the tenors

SECOND VOICE

and dogs bark blue in the face.

FIRST VOICE

Mrs Ogmore-Pritchard belches in a teeny hanky and chases the sunlight with a flywhisk, but even she cannot drive out the Spring: from one of the finger-bowls a primrose grows.

SECOND VOICE

Mrs Dai Bread One and Mrs Dai Bread Two are sitting outside their house in Donkey Lane, one darkly one plumply blooming in the quick, dewy sun. Mrs Dai Bread Two is looking into a crystal ball which she holds in the lap of her dirty yellow petticoat, hard against her hard dark thighs.

MRS DAI BREAD TWO

Cross my palm with silver. Out of our housekeeping money. Aah!

MRS DAI BREAD ONE

What d'you see, lovie?

MRS DAI BREAD TWO

I see a featherbed. With three pillows on it. And a text above the bed. I can't read what it says, there's great clouds blowing. Now they have blown away. God is Love, the text says.

MRS DAI BREAD ONE (*Delighted*)

That's *our* bed.

MRS DAI BREAD TWO

And now it's vanished. The sun's spinning like a top. Who's this coming out of the sun? It's a hairy little man with big pink lips. He got a wall eye.

MRS DAI BREAD ONE

It's Dai, it's Dai Bread!

MRS DAI BREAD TWO

Ssh! The featherbed's floating back. The little man's taking his boots off. He's pulling his shirt over his head. He's beating his chest with his fists. He's climbing into bed.

MRS DAI BREAD ONE

Go on, go on.

MRS DAI BREAD TWO

There's *two* women in bed. He looks at them both, with his head cocked on one side. He's whistling through his teeth. Now he grips his little arms round one of the women.

MRS DAI BREAD ONE

Which one, which one?

MRS DAI BREAD TWO

I can't see any more. There's great clouds blowing again.

MRS DAI BREAD ONE

Ach, the mean old clouds!

[*Pause. The children's singing fades*]

FIRST VOICE

The morning is all singing. The Reverend Eli Jenkins, busy on his morning calls, stops outside the Welfare Hall to hear Polly Garter as she scrubs the floors for the Mothers' Union Dance tonight.

POLLY GARTER (*Singing*)

I loved a man whose name was Tom
He was strong as a bear and two yards long
I loved a man whose name was Dick
He was big as a barrel and three feet thick
And I loved a man whose name was Harry
Six feet tall and sweet as a cherry
But the one I loved best awake or asleep
Was little Willy Wee and he's six feet deep.

O Tom Dick and Harry were three fine men
And I'll never have such loving again
But little Willy Wee who took me on his knee
Little Willy Wee was the man for me.

Now men from every parish round
Run after me and roll me on the ground
But whenever I love another man back
Johnnie from the Hill or Sailing Jack
I always think as they do what they please
Of Tom Dick and Harry who were tall as trees
And most I think when I'm by their side
Of little Willy Wee who downed and died.

O Tom Dick and Harry were three fine men
And I'll never have such loving again
But little Willy Wee who took me on his knee
Little Willy Weazel is the man for me.

REV. ELI JENKINS

Praise the Lord! We are a musical nation.

SECOND VOICE

And the Reverend Jenkins hurries on through the town to visit the sick with jelly and poems.

FIRST VOICE

The town's as full as a lovebird's egg.

MR WALDO

There goes the Reverend,

FIRST VOICE

says Mr Waldo at the smoked herring brown window of the unwashed Sailors Arms,

MR WALDO

with his brolly and his odes. Fill 'em up, Sinbad, I'm on the treacle today.

SECOND VOICE

The silent fishermen flush down their pints.

SINBAD

Oh, Mr Waldo,

sighs Sinbad Sailors,

SINBAD

I dote on that Gossamer Beynon. She's a lady all over.

FIRST VOICE

And Mr Waldo, who is thinking of a woman soft as Eve
and sharp as sciatica to share his bread-pudding bed, answers

MR WALDO

No lady that I know is.

SINBAD

And if only grandma'd die, cross my heart I'd go down
on my knees Mr Waldo and I'd say Miss Gossamer I'd say

CHILDREN'S VOICES

When birds do sing hey ding a ding a ding
Sweet lovers love the Spring . . .

SECOND VOICE

Polly Garter sings, still on her knees,

POLLY GARTER

Tom Dick and Harry were three fine men
And I'll never have such

CHILDREN

ding a ding

POLLY GARTER

again.

FIRST VOICE

And the morning school is over, and Captain Cat at his curtained schooner's porthole open to the Spring sun tides hears the naughty forfeiting children tumble and rhyme on the cobbles.

GIRLS' VOICES

Gwennie call the boys
They make such a noise.

GIRL

Boys boys boys
Come along to me.

GIRLS' VOICES

Boys boys boys
Kiss Gwennie where she says
Or give her a penny.
Go on, Gwennie.

GIRL

Kiss me in Goosegog Lane

Or give me a penny.
What's your name?

FIRST BOY

Billy.

GIRL

Kiss me in Goosegog Lane Billy
Or give me a penny silly.

FIRST BOY

Gwennie Gwennie
I kiss you in Goosegog Lane.
Now I haven't got to give you a penny.

GIRLS' VOICES

Boys boys boys
Kiss Gwennie where she says
Or give her a penny.
Go on, Gwennie.

GIRL

Kiss me on Llareggub Hill
Or give me a penny.
What's your name?

SECOND BOY

Johnnie Cristo.

· 73 ·

GIRL

Kiss me on Llareggub Hill Johnnie Cristo
Or give me a penny mister.

SECOND BOY

Gwennie Gwennie
I kiss you on Llareggub Hill.
Now I haven't got to give you a penny.

GIRLS' VOICES

Boys boys boys
Kiss Gwennie where she says
Or give her a penny.
Go on, Gwennie.

GIRL

Kiss me in Milk Wood
Or give me a penny.
What's your name?

THIRD BOY

Dicky.

GIRL

Kiss me in Milk Wood Dicky
Or give me a penny quickly.

Gwennie Gwennie
I can't kiss you in Milk Wood.

GIRLS' VOICES
Gwennie ask him why.

GIRL
Why?

THIRD BOY
Because my mother says I mustn't.

GIRLS' VOICES
Cowardy cowardy custard
Give Gwennie a penny.

GIRL
Give me a penny.

THIRD BOY
I haven't got any.

GIRLS' VOICES
Put him in the river
Up to his liver
Quick quick Dirty Dick

Beat him on the bum
With a rhubarb stick.
Aiee!
Hush!

FIRST VOICE

And the shrill girls giggle and master around him and squeal as they clutch and thrash, and he blubbers away downhill with his patched pants falling, and his tear-splashed blush burns all the way as the triumphant bird-like sisters scream with buttons in their claws and the bully brothers hoot after him his little nickname and his mother's shame and his father's wickedness with the loose wild barefoot women of the hovels of the hills. It all means nothing at all, and, howling for his milky mum, for her cawl and buttermilk and cowbreath and welshcakes and the fat birth-smelling bed and moonlit kitchen of her arms, he'll never forget as he paddles blind home through the weeping end of the world. Then his tormentors tussle and run to the Cockle Street sweet-shop, their pennies sticky as honey, to buy from Miss Myfanwy Price, who is cocky and neat as a puff-bosomed robin and her small round buttocks tight as ticks, gobstoppers big as wens that rainbow as you suck, brandyballs, winegums, hundreds and thousands, liquorice sweet as sick, nougat to tug and ribbon out like another red rubbery tongue, gum to glue in girls' curls, crimson coughdrops to spit blood, ice-cream cornets, dandelion-and-burdock, raspberry and cherryade, pop goes the weasel and the wind.

SECOND VOICE

Gossamer Beynon high-heels out of school. The sun hums down through the cotton flowers of her dress into the bell of her heart and buzzes in the honey there and couches and kisses, lazy-loving and boozed, in her red-berried breast. Eyes run from the trees and windows of the street, steaming 'Gossamer', and strip her to the nipples and the bees. She blazes naked past the Sailors Arms, the only woman on the Dai-Adamed earth. Sinbad Sailors places on her thighs still dewdamp from the first mangrowing cock-crow garden his reverent goat-bearded hands.

GOSSAMER BEYNON

I don't care if he *is* common,

SECOND VOICE

she whispers to her salad-day deep self,

GOSSAMER BEYNON

I want to gobble him up. I don't care if he *does* drop his aitches,

SECOND VOICE

she tells the stripped and mother-of-the-world big-beamed and Eve-hipped spring of her self, so long as he's all cucumber and hooves.

SECOND VOICE

Sinbad Sailors watches her go by, demure and proud and schoolmarm in her crisp flower dress and sun-defying hat, with never a look or lilt or wriggle, the butcher's unmelting icemaiden daughter veiled for ever from the hungry hug of his eyes.

SINBAD SAILORS

Oh, Gossamer Beynon, why are you so proud?

SECOND VOICE

he grieves to his guinness,

SINBAD SAILORS

Oh, beautiful beautiful Gossamer B, I wish I wish that you were for me. I wish you were not so educated.

SECOND VOICE

She feels his goatbeard tickle her in the middle of the world like a tuft of wiry fire, and she turns in a terror of delight away from his whips and whiskery conflagration, and sits down in the kitchen to a plate heaped high with chips and the kidneys of lambs.

In the blind-drawn dark dining-room of School House, dusty and echoing as a dining-room in a vault, Mr and Mrs Pugh are silent over cold grey cottage pie. Mr Pugh reads, as he forks the shroud meat in, from *Lives of the Great Poisoners*. He has bound a plain brown-paper cover round the book. Slyly, between slow mouthfuls, he sidespies up at Mrs Pugh, poisons her with his eye, then goes on reading. He underlines certain passages and smiles in secret.

MRS PUGH

Persons with manners do not read at table,

FIRST VOICE

says Mrs Pugh. She swallows a digestive tablet as big as a horse-pill, washing it down with clouded peasoup water.

[*Pause*]

MRS PUGH

Some persons were brought up in pigsties.

MR PUGH

Pigs don't read at table, dear.

FIRST VOICE

Bitterly she flicks dust from the broken cruet It settles on the pie in a thin gnat-rain.

MR PUGH

Pigs can't read, my dear.

MRS PUGH

I know one who can.

FIRST VOICE

Alone in the hissing laboratory of his wishes, Mr Pugh minces among bad vats and jeroboams, tiptoes through spinneys of murdering herbs, agony dancing in his crucibles, and mixes especially for Mrs Pugh a venomous porridge unknown to toxicologists which will scald and viper through her until her ears fall off like figs, her toes grow big and black as balloons, and steam comes screaming out of her navel.

MR PUGH

You know best, dear,

FIRST VOICE

says Mr Pugh, and quick as a flash he ducks her in rat soup.

MRS PUGH

What's that book by your trough, Mr Pugh?

MR PUGH

It's a theological work, my dear. *Lives of the Great Saints*.

FIRST VOICE

Mrs Pugh smiles. An icicle forms in the cold air of the dining-vault.

MRS PUGH

I saw you talking to a saint this morning. Saint Polly Garter. She was martyred again last night. Mrs Organ Morgan saw her with Mr Waldo.

MRS ORGAN MORGAN

And when they saw me they pretended they were looking for nests,

SECOND VOICE

said Mrs Organ Morgan to her husband, with her mouth full of fish as a pelican's.

MRS ORGAN MORGAN

But you don't go nesting in long combinations, I said to myself, like Mr Waldo was wearing, and your dress nearly over your head like Polly Garter's. Oh, they didn't fool me.

SECOND VOICE

One big bird gulp, and the flounder's gone. She licks her lips and goes stabbing again.

MRS ORGAN MORGAN

And when you think of all those babies she's got, then all I can say is she'd better give up bird nesting that's all I can say, it isn't the right kind of hobby at all for a woman that can't say No even to midgets. Remember Bob Spit? He wasn't any bigger than a baby and he gave her two. But they're two nice boys, I will say that, Fred Spit and Arthur. Sometimes I like Fred best and sometimes I like Arthur. Who do you like best, Organ?

ORGAN MORGAN

Oh, Bach without any doubt. Bach every time for me.

MRS ORGAN MORGAN

Organ Morgan, you haven't been listening to a word I said. It's organ organ all the time with you . . .

FIRST VOICE

And she bursts into tears, and, in the middle of her salty howling, nimbly spears a small flatfish and pelicans it whole.

ORGAN MORGAN

And then Palestrina,

SECOND VOICE

says Organ Morgan.

FIRST VOICE

Lord Cut-Glass, in his kitchen full of time, squats down alone to a dogdish, marked Fido, of peppery fish-scraps and listens to the voices of his sixty-six clocks, one for each year of his loony age, and watches, with love, their black-and-white moony loudlipped faces tocking the earth away: slow clocks, quick clocks, pendulumed heart-knocks, china, alarm, grandfather, cuckoo; clocks shaped like Noah's whirring Ark, clocks that bicker in marble ships, clocks in the wombs of glass women, hourglass chimers, tu-wit-tu-woo clocks, clocks that pluck tunes, Vesuvius clocks all black bells and lava, Niagara clocks that cataract their ticks, old time-weeping clocks with ebony beards, clocks with no hands for ever drumming out time without ever knowing what time it is. His sixty-six singers are all set at different hours. Lord Cut-Glass lives in a house and a life at siege. Any minute or dark day now, the unknown enemy will loot and savage downhill, but they will not catch him napping. Sixty-six different times in his fish-slimy kitchen ping, strike, tick, chime, and tock.

SECOND VOICE

The lust and lilt and lather and emerald breeze and crackle of the bird-praise and body of Spring with its breasts full of rivering May-milk, means, to that lordly fish-head nibbler, nothing but another nearness to the tribes and navies of the Last Black Day who'll sear and pillage down Armageddon Hill to his double-locked rusty-shuttered tick-tock dust-scrabbled shack at the bottom of the town that has fallen head over bells in love.

POLLY GARTER

And I'll never have such loving again,

SECOND VOICE

pretty Polly hums and longs.

POLLY GARTER (*Sings*)

Now when farmers' boys on the first fair day
Come down from the hills to drink and be gay,
Before the sun sinks I'll lie there in their arms
For they're *good* bad boys from the lonely farms,

But I always think as we tumble into bed
Of little Willy Wee who is dead, dead, dead . . .

[*A silence*]

FIRST VOICE

The sunny slow lulling afternoon yawns and moons through the dozy town. The sea lolls, laps and idles in, with fishes sleeping in its lap. The meadows still as Sunday, the shut-eye tasselled bulls, the goat-and-daisy dingles, nap happy and lazy. The dumb duck-ponds snooze. Clouds sag and pillow on Llareggub Hill. Pigs grunt in a wet wallow-bath, and smile as they snort and dream. They dream of the acorned swill of the world, the rooting for pig-fruit, the bagpipe dugs of the mother sow, the squeal and snuffle of yesses of the women pigs in rut. They mud-bask and snout in the pig-loving sun; their tails curl; they rollick and slobber and snore to deep, smug, after-swill sleep. Donkeys angelically drowse on Donkey Down.

MRS PUGH

Persons with manners,

SECOND VOICE

snaps Mrs cold Pugh,

MRS PUGH

do not nod at table.

FIRST VOICE

Mr Pugh cringes awake. He puts on a soft-soaping smile: it is sad and grey under his nicotine-eggyellow weeping walrus Victorian moustache worn thick and long in memory of Doctor Crippen.

MRS PUGH

You should wait until you retire to your sty,

SECOND VOICE

says Mrs Pugh, sweet as a razor. His fawning measly quarter-smile freezes. Sly and silent, he foxes into his chemist's den and there, in a hiss and prussic circle of cauldrons and phials brimful with pox and the Black Death, cooks up a fricassee of deadly nightshade, nicotine, hot frog, cyanide and bat-spit for his needling stalactite hag and bednag of a poker-backed nutcracker wife.

MR PUGH

I beg your pardon, my dear,

SECOND VOICE

he murmurs with a wheedle.

FIRST VOICE

Captain Cat, at his window thrown wide to the sun and the clippered seas he sailed long ago when his eyes were blue and bright, slumbers and voyages; ear-ringed and rolling, I Love You Rosie Probert tattooed on his belly, he brawls with broken bottles in the fug and babel of the dark dock bars, roves with a herd of short and good time cows in every naughty port and twines and souses with the drowned and blowzy-breasted dead. He weeps as he sleeps and sails.

SECOND VOICE

One voice of all he remembers most dearly as his dream buckets down. Lazy early Rosie with the flaxen thatch, whom he shared with Tom-Fred the donkeyman and many

another seaman, clearly and near to him speaks from the bedroom of her dust. In that gulf and haven, fleets by the dozen
have anchored for the little heaven of the night; but she
speaks to Captain napping Cat alone. Mrs Probert . . .

ROSIE PROBERT
from Duck Lane, Jack. Quack twice and ask for Rosie

SECOND VOICE
. . . is the one love of his sea-life that was sardined with
women.

ROSIE PROBERT (*Softly*)
What seas did you see,
Tom Cat, Tom Cat,
In your sailoring days
Long long ago?
What sea beasts were
In the wavery green
When you were my master?

CAPTAIN CAT
I'll tell you the truth.
Seas barking like seals,
Blue seas and green,
Seas covered with eels
And mermen and whales.

ROSIE PROBERT

What seas did you sail
Old whaler when
On the blubbery waves
Between Frisco and Wales
You were my bosun?

CAPTAIN CAT

As true as I'm here
Dear you Tom Cat's tart
You landlubber Rosie
You cosy love
My easy as easy
My true sweetheart,
Seas green as a bean
Seas gliding with swans
In the seal-barking moon.

ROSIE PROBERT

What seas were rocking
My little deck hand
My favourite husband
In your seaboots and hunger
My duck my whaler
My honey my daddy
My pretty sugar sailor
With my name on your belly

When you were a boy
Long long ago?

CAPTAIN CAT

I'll tell you no lies.
The only sea I saw
Was the seesaw sea
With you riding on it.
Lie down, lie easy.
Let me shipwreck in your thighs.

ROSIE PROBERT

Knock twice, Jack,
At the door of my grave
And ask for Rosie.

CAPTAIN CAT

Rosie Probert.

ROSIE PROBERT

Remember her.
She is forgetting.
The earth which filled her mouth
Is vanishing from her.
Remember me.
I have forgotten you.
I am going into the darkness of the darkness for ever.
I have forgotten that I was ever born.

CHILD

Look,

FIRST VOICE

says a child to her mother as they pass by the window of
Schooner House,

CHILD

Captain Cat is crying

FIRST VOICE

Captain Cat is crying

CAPTAIN CAT

Come back, come back,

FIRST VOICE

up the silences and echoes of the passages of the eternal
night.

CHILD

He's crying all over his nose,

FIRST VOICE

says the child. Mother and child move on down the street.

CHILD

He's got a nose like strawberries,

the child says; and then she forgets him too. She sees in the still middle of the bluebagged bay Nogood Boyo fishing from the *Zanzibar*.

CHILD

Nogood Boyo gave me three pennies yesterday but I wouldn't,

FIRST VOICE

the child tells her mother.

SECOND VOICE

Boyo catches a whalebone corset. It is all he has caught all day.

NOGOOD BOYO

Bloody funny fish!

SECOND VOICE

Mrs Dai Bread Two gypsies up his mind's slow eye, dressed only in a bangle.

NOGOOD BOYO

She's wearing her nightgown. (*Pleadingly*) Would you like this nice wet corset, Mrs Dai Bread Two?

MRS DAI BREAD TWO

No, I *won't*!

NOGOOD BOYO

And a bite of my little apple?

SECOND VOICE

he offers with no hope.

FIRST VOICE

She shakes her brass nightgown, and he chases her out of his mind; and when he comes gusting back, there in the bloodshot centre of his eye a geisha girl grins and bows in a kimono of ricepaper.

NOGOOD BOYO

I want to be *good* Boyo, but nobody'll let me,

FIRST VOICE

he sighs as she writhes politely. The land fades, the sea flocks silently away; and through the warm white cloud where he lies, silky, tingling, uneasy Eastern music undoes him in a Japanese minute.

SECOND VOICE

The afternoon buzzes like lazy bees round the flowers round Mae Rose Cottage. Nearly asleep in the field of nannygoats who hum and gently butt the sun, she blows love on a puffball.

> MAE ROSE COTTAGE (*Lazily*)
> He loves me
> He loves me not
> He loves me
> He loves me not
> He *loves* me!—the dirty old fool.

SECOND VOICE

Lazy she lies alone in clover and sweet-grass, seventeen and never been sweet in the grass ho ho.

FIRST VOICE

The Reverend Eli Jenkins inky in his cool front parlour or poem-room tells only the truth in his Lifework—the Population, Main Industry, Shipping, History, Topography, Flora and Fauna of the town he worships in—the White Book of Llareggub. Portraits of famous bards and preachers, all fur and wool from the squint to the kneecaps, hang over him heavy as sheep, next to faint lady watercolours of pale green Milk Wood like a lettuce salad dying. His mother, propped against a pot in a palm, with her wedding-ring waist and bust like a black-clothed dining-table suffers in her stays.

REV. ELI JENKINS

Oh angels be careful there with your knives and forks,

he prays. There is no known likeness of his father Esau, who, undogcollared because of his little weakness, was scythed to the bone one harvest by mistake when sleeping with his weakness in the corn. He lost all ambition and died, with one leg.

REV. ELI JENKINS

Poor Dad,

SECOND VOICE

grieves the Reverend Eli,

REV. ELI JENKINS

to die of drink and agriculture.

SECOND VOICE

Farmer Watkins in Salt Lake Farm hates his cattle on the hill as he ho's them in to milking.

UTAH WATKINS (*In a fury*)

Damn you, you damned dairies!

SECOND VOICE

A cow kisses him.

UTAH WATKINS

Bite her to death!

he shouts to his deaf dog who smiles and licks his hands.

UTAH WATKINS

Gore him, sit on him, Daisy!

SECOND VOICE

he bawls to the cow who barbed him with her tongue, and she moos gentle words as he raves and dances among his summerbreathed slaves walking delicately to the farm. The coming of the end of the Spring day is already reflected in the lakes of their great eyes. Bessie Bighead greets them by the names she gave them when they were maidens.

BESSIE BIGHEAD

Peg, Meg, Buttercup, Moll,
Fan from the Castle,
Theodosia and Daisy.

SECOND VOICE

They bow their heads.

FIRST VOICE

Look up Bessie Bighead in the White Book of Llareggub and you will find the few haggard rags and the one poor glittering thread of her history laid out in pages there with as much love and care as the lock of hair of a first lost love.

Conceived in Milk Wood, born in a barn, wrapped in paper, left on a doorstep, bigheaded and bass-voiced she grew in the dark until long-dead Gomer Owen kissed her when she wasn't looking because he was dared. Now in the light she'll work, sing, milk, say the cows' sweet names and sleep until the night sucks out her soul and spits it into the sky. In her life-long love light, holily Bessie milks the fond lake-eyed cows as dusk showers slowly down over byre, sea and town.

Utah Watkins curses through the farmyard on a carthorse.

UTAH WATKINS
Gallop, you bleeding cripple!

FIRST VOICE
and the huge horse neighs softly as though he had given it a lump of sugar.

Now the town is dusk. Each cobble, donkey, goose and gooseberry street is a thoroughfare of dusk; and dusk and ceremonial dust, and night's first darkening snow, and the sleep of birds, drift under and through the live dusk of this place of love. Llareggub is the capital of dusk.

Mrs Ogmore-Pritchard, at the first drop of the dusk-shower, seals all her sea-view doors, draws the germ-free blinds, sits, erect as a dry dream on a high-backed hygienic chair and wills herself to cold, quick sleep. At once, at twice, Mr Ogmore and Mr Pritchard, who all dead day long have been gossiping like ghosts in the woodshed, planning the loveless destruction of their glass widow, reluctantly sigh and sidle into her clean house.

MR PRITCHARD

You first, Mr Ogmore.

MR OGMORE

After you, Mr Pritchard.

MR PRITCHARD

No, no, Mr Ogmore. You widowed her first.

FIRST VOICE

And in through the keyhole, with tears where their eyes once were, they ooze and grumble.

MRS OGMORE-PRITCHARD

Husbands,

FIRST VOICE

she says in her sleep. There is acid love in her voice for one of the two shambling phantoms. Mr Ogmore hopes that it is not for him. So does Mr Pritchard.

MRS OGMORE-PRITCHARD

I love you both.

MR OGMORE (*With terror*)

Oh, Mrs Ogmore.

MR PRITCHARD (*With horror*)

Oh, Mrs Pritchard.

MRS OGMORE-PRITCHARD

Soon it will be time to go to bed. Tell me your tasks in order.

MR OGMORE AND MR PRITCHARD

We must take our pyjamas from the drawer marked pyjamas.

MRS OGMORE-PRITCHARD (*Coldly*)

And then you must take them off.

SECOND VOICE

Down in the dusking town, Mae Rose Cottage, still lying in clover, listens to the nannygoats chew, draws circles of lipstick round her nipples.

MAE ROSE COTTAGE

I'm *fast*. I'm a bad lot. God will strike me dead. I'm seventeen. I'll go to hell,

SECOND VOICE

she tells the goats.

You just wait. I'll sin till I blow up!

SECOND VOICE

She lies deep, waiting for the worst to happen; the goats champ and sneer.

FIRST VOICE

And at the doorway of Bethesda House, the Reverend Jenkins recites to Llareggub Hill his sunset poem.

REV. ELI JENKINS

Every morning when I wake,
Dear Lord, a little prayer I make,
O please to keep Thy lovely eye
On all poor creatures born to die.

And every evening at sun-down
I ask a blessing on the town,
For whether we last the night or no
I'm sure is always touch-and-go.

We are not wholly bad or good
Who live our lives under Milk Wood,
And Thou, I know, wilt be the first
To see our best side, not our worst.

O let us see another day!
Bless us this night, I pray,
And to the sun we all will bow
And say, good-bye—but just for now!

FIRST VOICE

Jack Black prepares once more to meet his Satan in the Wood. He grinds his night-teeth, closes his eyes, climbs into his religious trousers, their flies sewn up with cobbler's thread, and pads out, torched and bibled, grimly, joyfully, into the already sinning dusk.

JACK BLACK

Off to Gomorrah!

SECOND VOICE

And Lily Smalls is up to Nogood Boyo in the wash-house.

FIRST VOICE

And Cherry Owen, sober as Sunday as he is every day of the week, goes off happy as Saturday to get drunk as a deacon as he does every night.

CHERRY OWEN

I always say she's got two husbands,

FIRST VOICE

says Cherry Owen,

CHERRY OWEN

one drunk and one sober.

FIRST VOICE

And Mrs Cherry simply says

MRS CHERRY OWEN

And aren't I a lucky woman? Because I love them both.

SINBAD

Evening, Cherry.

CHERRY OWEN

Evening, Sinbad.

SINBAD

What'll you have?

CHERRY OWEN

Too much.

SINBAD

The Sailors Arms is always open . . .

FIRST VOICE

Sinbad suffers to himself, heartbroken,

SINBAD

. . . oh, Gossamer, open yours!

FIRST VOICE

Dusk is drowned for ever until tomorrow. It is all at once night now. The windy town is a hill of windows, and from the larrupped waves the lights of the lamps in the windows call back the day and the dead that have run away to sea. All over the calling dark, babies and old men are bribed and lullabied to sleep.

FIRST WOMAN'S VOICE

Hushabye, baby, the sandman is coming . . .

SECOND WOMAN'S VOICE (*Singing*)

Rockabye, grandpa, in the tree top,
When the wind blows the cradle will rock,
When the bough breaks the cradle will fall,
Down will come grandpa, whiskers and all.

FIRST VOICE

Or their daughters cover up the old unwinking men like parrots, and in their little dark in the lit and bustling young kitchen corners, all night long they watch, beady-eyed, the long night through in case death catches them asleep.

SECOND VOICE

Unmarried girls, alone in their privately bridal bedrooms, powder and curl for the Dance of the World.

[*Accordion music: dim*]

They make, in front of their looking-glasses, haughty or
come-hithering faces for the young men in the street outside,
at the lamplit leaning corners, who wait in the all-at-once
wind to wolve and whistle.

[*Accordion music louder, then fading under*]

FIRST VOICE

The drinkers in the Sailors Arms drink to the failure of
the dance.

A DRINKER

Down with the waltzing and the skipping.

CHERRY OWEN

Dancing isn't natural,

FIRST VOICE

righteously says Cherry Owen who has just downed
seventeen pints of flat, warm, thin, Welsh, bitter beer.

SECOND VOICE

A farmer's lantern glimmers, a spark on Llareggub hillside.

[*Accordion music fades into silence*]

Llareggub Hill, writes the Reverend Jenkins in his poem-room,

REV. ELI JENKINS
Llareggub Hill, that mystic tumulus, the memorial of peoples that dwelt in the region of Llareggub before the Celts left the Land of Summer and where the old wizards made themselves a wife out of flowers.

SECOND VOICE
Mr Waldo, in his corner of the Sailors Arms, sings:

MR WALDO
In Pembroke City when I was young
I lived by the Castle Keep
Sixpence a week was my wages
For working for the chimbley sweep.
Six cold pennies he gave me
Not a farthing more or less
And all the fare I could afford
Was parsnip gin and watercress.
I did not need a knife and fork
Or a bib up to my chin
To dine on a dish of watercress
And a jug of parsnip gin.
Did you ever hear a growing boy

To live so cruel cheap
On grub that has no flesh and bones
And liquor that makes you weep?
Sweep sweep chimbley sweep,
I wept through Pembroke City
Poor and barefoot in the snow
Till a kind young woman took pity.
Poor little chimbley sweep she said
Black as the ace of spades
O nobody's swept my chimbley
Since my husband went his ways.
Come and sweep my chimbley
Come and sweep my chimbley
She sighed to me with a blush
Come and sweep my chimbley
Come and sweep my chimbley
Bring along your chimbley brush!

FIRST VOICE

Blind Captain Cat climbs into his bunk. Like a cat, he sees in the dark. Through the voyages of his tears he sails to see the dead.

CAPTAIN CAT

Dancing Williams!

FIRST DROWNED

Still dancing.

CAPTAIN CAT

Jonah Jarvis

THIRD DROWNED

Still.

FIRST DROWNED

Curly Bevan's skull.

ROSIE PROBERT

Rosie, with God. She has forgotten dying.

FIRST VOICE

The dead come out in their Sunday best.

SECOND VOICE

Listen to the night breaking.

FIRST VOICE

Organ Morgan goes to chapel to play the organ. He sees Bach lying on a tombstone.

ORGAN MORGAN

Johann Sebastian!

CHERRY OWEN (*Drunkenly*)

Who?

ORGAN MORGAN

Johann Sebastian mighty Bach. Oh, Bach fach.

CHERRY OWEN

To hell with you,

FIRST VOICE

says Cherry Owen who is resting on the tombstone on his way home.

Mr Mog Edwards and Miss Myfanwy Price happily apart from one another at the top and the sea end of the town write their everynight letters of love and desire. In the warm White Book of Llareggub you will find the little maps of the islands of their contentment.

MYFANWY PRICE

Oh, my Mog, I am yours for ever.

FIRST VOICE

And she looks around with pleasure at her own neat neverdull room which Mr Mog Edwards will never enter.

MOG EDWARDS

Come to my arms, Myfanwy.

FIRST VOICE

And he hugs his lovely money to his *own* heart.

And Mr Waldo drunk in the dusky wood hugs his lovely Polly Garter under the eyes and rattling tongues of the neighbours and the birds, and he does not care. He smacks his live red lips.

But it is not *his* name that Polly Garter whispers as she lies under the oak and loves him back. Six feet deep that name sings in the cold earth.

POLLY GARTER (*Sings*)
But I always think as we tumble into bed
Of little Willy Wee who is dead, dead, dead.

FIRST VOICE

The thin night darkens. A breeze from the creased water sighs the streets close under Milk waking Wood. The Wood, whose every tree-foot's cloven in the black glad sight of the hunters of lovers, that is a God-built garden to Mary Ann Sailors who knows there is Heaven on earth and the chosen people of His kind fire in Llareggub's land, that is the fairday farmhands' wantoning ignorant chapel of bridesbeds, and, to the Reverend Eli Jenkins, a greenleaved sermon on the innocence of men, the suddenly windshaken wood springs awake for the second dark time this one Spring day.

NOTES ON PRONUNCIATION

[Page 2] *Rhiannon:* strongly aspirated *r*, and accent on the second syllable. *Llareggub:* a voiceless *l* produced from the side of the mouth, accent on the second syllable, the third syllable rhyming with 'bib'. *Dai:* as 'dye'.

[Page 7, 8] *Dowlais:* accent on the first syllable, the second syllable rhyming with 'ice'. *Maesgwyn:* mice-gwin, accent on the second syllable. *Myfanwy:* accent on the second syllable, *f* as *v*, the first *y* an indeterminate sound, the second *v* as *ee*.

[Page 10] *Ach y fi:* the *ch* guttural, the *y* indeterminate, *f* as *v*, the whole pronounced as one word; an interjection expressing disgust.

[Page 16] *mwchins:* a compromise between the English 'mooching' and the Welsh dialect word 'mitching', playing truant.

[Page 26, 27] *Eisteddfodau:* eye-steth-vod-eye, the *th* voiced, a strong accent on the third syllable. *Parchs:* the *ch* guttural; clergymen.

[Page 28] *Organ Morgan:* the *r*'s rolled, the *o*'s short. *Gippo:* gipsy.

[Page 30] *Dewi:* de-wee; the first syllable, which has the accent, is short.

[Page 32] *Moel yr Wyddfa:* moil-er-ooithva, the *th* voiced. *Carnedd:* the *dd* a voiced *th,* the *r* rolled, accent on the first syllable.

[Page 32] *Penmaenmawr:* 'maen' rhymes with 'line', 'mawr' with 'hour'. *Sawdde:* southay, the *th* voiced. *Edw:* aid-oo. *Llyfnant:* *y* indeterminate, *f* as *v*. *Claerwen, Cleddau, Dulais:* clire-wen; cleth-eye, the *th* voiced; dill-ice. *Ogwr:* ogoorr, accent on the first syllable. *Cennen:* the *c* hard.

[Page 49] *Gerwain:* gerr-wine, the *g* hard. *Ty*: as 'tee'.

[Page 52] *Gorslas:* gorse-lahss, with a strong accent on the second syllable.

[Page 63] *Twll:* ooll, the *oo* short, the *ll* as in 'Llareggub'.

[Page 76] *cawl:* as 'cowl'; a broth with leeks.

[Page 107] *fach:* an expression of endearment; *f* as *v*, and the *ch* guttural.

FIRST BROADCAST

FULL CAST

First Voice	*Richard Burton*
Second Voice	*Richard Bebb*
Captain Cat	*Hugh Griffith*
First Drowned	*Dillwyn Owen*
Second Drowned	*Meredith Edwards*
Rosie Probert	*Rachel Thomas*
Third Drowned	*John Huw Jones*
Fourth Drowned	*Philip Burton*
Fifth Drowned	*John Ormond Thomas*
Mr Mog Edwards	*Dafydd Havard*
Miss Myfanwy Price	*Sybil Williams*
Jack Black	*John Glyn Jones*
Waldo's Mother	*Olwen Brookes*
Little Boy Waldo	*Diana Maddox*
Waldo's Wife	*Mary Jones*
Mr Waldo	*Meredith Edwards*
First Neighbour	*Dilys Davies*
Second Neighbour	*Rachel Roberts*

Third Neighbour	*Lorna Davies*
Fourth Neighbour	*Gwenllian Owen*
Matti's Mother	*Rachel Thomas*
First Woman	*Rachel Roberts*
Second Woman	*Sybil Williams*
Third Woman	*Gwyneth Petty*
Fourth Woman	*Olwen Brookes*
Fifth Woman	*Lorna Davies*
Preacher	*Philip Burton*
Mrs Ogmore-Pritchard	*Dilys Davies*
Mr Ogmore	*David Close-Thomas*
Mr Pritchard	*Ben Williams*
Gossamer Beynon	*Gwenllian Owen*
Organ Morgan	*John Glyn Jones*
Utah Watkins	*Meredith Edwards*
Mrs Utah Watkins	*Rachel Thomas*
Ocky Milkman	*Dillwyn Owen*
A Voice	*John Huw Jones*
Mrs Willy Nilly	*Rachel Thomas*
Lily Smalls	*Gwyneth Petty*
Mae Rose Cottage	*Rachel Roberts*
Butcher Beynon	*Meredith Edwards*
Rev. Eli Jenkins	*Philip Burton*
Mr Pugh	*John Huw Jones*
Mrs Organ Morgan	*Olwen Brookes*
Mary Ann Sailors	*Rachel Thomas*
Dai Bread	*David Close-Thomas*

Polly Garter	*Diana Maddox*
Nogood Boyo	*Dillwyn Owen*
Lord Cut-Glass	*John Glyn Jones*
Gwennie	*Norma Jones*
Mrs Beynon	*Olwen Brookes*
Mrs Pugh	*Mary Jones*
Mrs Dai Bread One	*Gwyneth Petty*
Mrs Dai Bread Two	*Rachel Roberts*
Willy Nilly	*Ben Williams*
Mrs Cherry Owen	*Lorna Davies*
Cherry Owen	*John Ormond Thomas*
Sinbad	*Aubrey Richards*
Old Man	*David Close-Thomas*
First Neighbour	*Gwyneth Petty*
Second Neighbour	*Sybil Williams*
Third Neighbour	*Lorna Davies*
Fourth Neighbour	*Mary Jones*
Evans the Death	*Meredith Edwards*
Fisherman	*Dillwyn Owen*
Child	*Norma Jones*
Bessie Bighead	*Gwyneth Petty*
First Woman	*Gwenllian Owen*
Second Woman	*Rachel Roberts*
A Drinker	*Dafydd Havard*

Children of Laugharne School, Carmarthenshire

VINTAGE CLASSICS

Vintage launched in the United Kingdom in 1990, and was originally the paperback home for the Random House Group's literary authors. Now, Vintage comprises some of London's oldest and most prestigious literary houses, including Chatto & Windus (1855), Hogarth (1917), Jonathan Cape (1921) and Secker & Warburg (1935), alongside the newer or relaunched hardback and paperback imprints: The Bodley Head, Harvill Secker, Yellow Jersey, Square Peg, Vintage Paperbacks and Vintage Classics.

From Angela Carter, Graham Greene and Aldous Huxley to Toni Morrison, Haruki Murakami and Virginia Woolf, Vintage Classics is renowned for publishing some of the greatest writers and thinkers from around the world and across the ages – all complemented by our beautiful, stylish approach to design. Vintage Classics' authors have won many of the world's most revered literary prizes, including the Nobel, the Booker, the Prix Goncourt and the Pulitzer, and through their writing they continue to capture imaginations, inspire new perspectives and incite curiosity.

In 2007 Vintage Classics introduced its distinctive red spine design, and in 2012 Vintage Children's Classics was launched to include the much-loved authors of our childhood. Random House joined forces with the Penguin Group in 2013 to become Penguin Random House, making it the largest trade publisher in the United Kingdom.

@vintagebooks